Table Talk

Table Talk

Beginning the Conversation
on the Gospel of Matthew
(Year A)

Jay Cormier

New City Press
Hyde Park, New York

For Paul Dowd

Published in the United States by New City Press
202 Comforter Blvd., Hyde Park, NY 12538
www.newcitypress.com
©2010 Jay Cormier

Cover design by Durva Correia

   Library of Congress Cataloging-in-Publication Data:

A copy of the CIP data is available from the Library of Congress

ISBN 978-1-56548-352-1

Printed in the United States of America

Contents

The Easter Triduum

Easter

Solemnities of the Lord in Ordinary Time

Ordinary Time

Introduction

*T*his book is designed to begin a *conversation,* a conversation that takes place each Sunday at the table of the Lord.

The conversation begins with a particular memory of the extraordinary life of the Gospel Jesus: a story he told, a wonder he worked; a confrontation with the establishment, a misunderstanding with his disciples; remembering when he cried, when he despaired, when he was abandoned, when he got angry; the injustice of his condemnation, the horror of his death, the vindication of his resurrection.

The conversation then seeks to understand what this memory of Jesus means to us in the marketplaces and temples of our time and place. In word and sacrament, we share the wonders of healing and forgiveness that Jesus is performing in our midst.

It's a conversation that shows no signs of being exhausted.

It is the writer's hope that these pages will provoke *Table Talk* — reflection and insight about God's Word as it is proclaimed at the table of the Lord on Sunday. The focus here is on the Sunday Gospel — the climactic reading at the Sunday Eucharist in which God speaks to us, touches us, loves us in the story of Jesus, God's Christ, *Emmanuel.*

The reflections offered here are one poor pilgrim's attempt to grasp the Gospel after many journeys through the lectionary as a writer, teacher and struggling disciple. These essays are intended to help spark the Sunday conversation around your parish table: to be starting points for the homilist who will preach on the Gospel, the catechist who will teach that Gospel to children, the RCIA team who will lead candidates through a discussion of the passage, or the individual disciple looking for a companion on his/her day-to-day journey to Emmaus.

(This volume follows both the pericopes of both the Roman Catholic lectionary and the "common" lectionary used by many Protestant churches. Where different Gospel readings are assigned, reflections on each reading are offered).

The problem with a collection like this is that it might be perceived as a final word, a definitive reading, a complete analysis of the Sunday Gospel reading. This book is no such thing. It is one "converser's" reflection and best reading of these Gospel stories after many years of his own prayer, reflection and teaching. Perhaps you will find here few nuggets of gold from a very deep mine; more gifted and wiser miners will find much more of value as they dig deeper and deeper.

If this book helps you begin that conversation at your own table this Sunday or helps you in your own search and study, these pages will have done their job.

ADVENT

First Sunday of Advent

"Stay awake! For you do not know on which day your Lord will come."

Matthew 24: 37–44

Stay awake!

*I*t's a horrifying realization to make while you're driving: You've been asleep.

The rain, the monotonous rhythm of the windshield wipers, the endless miles of white highway markings lull you to sleep. Then, all of a sudden, you are startled by an oncoming car's headlights or a blasting truck horn. You discover that your car is veering into the opposite lane and heading straight for a guardrail or an embankment. Instantly you steer your car back into the center of your lane.

You are terrified. *How long was I asleep — a second, a minute, longer? God, what if I never saw that headlight or heard that horn?*

The rest of your trip is not the same. You pull over and stop. You calm down. You shake yourself into focus. The importance of your destination diminishes considerably. When you start out again, you're prepared with gum to chew, coffee to drink, and music to play — loud! — on the radio or CD. And, if at all possible, your window is opened wide.

You have a new, sobering awareness of where you are going and the dangers of your journey.

The season of Advent begins with Jesus' sobering warning — *Stay awake!* (a warning echoed by the Apostle Paul in his letter to the Romans, today's second reading). For Matthew's community, Christ's return as the judge of the living and the dead was imminent; the chilling images of today's Gospel are intended to call Matthew's church to vigilance for the end of this world and preparation for the beginning of the next — an event they believed they would see in their lifetimes. But today's Gospel can also be read/heard by the Church and Christians of every place and time as a sobering, unsettling reminder that this life of ours is indeed limited, that the moments we have been given are precious and few, that death is a reality all of us will one day face.

The First Sunday of Advent calls us to "stay awake" and not sleep through the opportunities life gives us to discover God and the things of God; these Advent days compel us to "watch," to pay attention to the signs of God's unmistakable presence in our lives.

*F*ather, Giver of this precious and wonderful life of ours,
wake us up to the preciousness of every moment
   you give us.
Do not let us sleep through the Advent we live every day.
May Christ's coming shake us awake
that we may come to know you in the love of others
and the goodness of this world you have given us.

Second Sunday of Advent

John the Baptist appeared, preaching in the desert of Judea, saying, "Repent, for the kingdom of heaven is at hand!"

Matthew 3: 1–12

Messengers

She is the first one at the shelter every morning. She opens up, changes and washes the bed linens, sweeps the floor and scrubs down the shower area. She quietly goes about her tasks with a joyful dedication that disarms visitors and often causes the staff to forget that she is a volunteer. In the dignity and compassion she extends to those who come to the shelter, she is a "messenger" of the love of God.

Saturday mornings are a special time for him. That's when he meets Kevin, his eleven-year-old "Little Brother." He says he gets as much out of his time with Kevin as Kevin does: the satisfaction that comes from being needed, the joy of giving to another — but to Kevin, his "Big Brother" is a "messenger" of hope.

She never imagined herself as an activist or a political *anything* before. She was happiest simply being "Mom." But that changed when her bright and beautiful seven-year-old was struck and killed by a drunk driver. Her pain and the pain of thousands of parents like her compelled her to speak out against the injustice and irresponsibility of deaths like her child's and to work for more effective laws and stricter penalties for those who drive impaired by drugs or alcohol. In her work for the safety of other children, she is a "messenger" of the justice of God.

These three "messengers" and the many like them who proclaim in their humility and compassion the Good News of God's presence in our midst mirror the ministry of John the Baptizer. John, who makes his Advent appearance in today's Gospel, calls us to embrace the meaning of our own baptism: compassion, for-giveness, justice, selflessness. The coming of Christ calls all of us to become his messenger — to proclaim to our world the good news of "Emmanuel" — God is in our midst.

Matthew's description of John recalls the austere dress of the great prophet Elijah (2 Kings 1: 8). The Jews believed that Elijah would return from heaven to announce the long-awaited restoration of Israel as God's kingdom. For Matthew, this expectation is fulfilled in John the Baptizer. The "Old" Testament touches the "New" in the figure of the Baptizer.

John challenges two of the ruling classes of the Jewish establishment.

The Pharisees ("separated ones") were a group of particularly observant and influential Jews, respected for their faithful keeping of the Torah in everyday life. Pharisees were often called upon to be judges and arbiters of such matters as ritual purity, food tithes and the Sabbath observance. In their belief in the resurrection and in free will, they were considered progressive in their theology.

Little is known of the Sadducees ("righteous ones"). They seem to have been an elite class of priests associated with the temple in Jerusalem. Although they are mentioned in tandem with the Pharisees as opponents of Jesus, the two groups were frequently at odds over matters of theology (the Sadducees rejected the idea of life after death). The Sadducees were especially influential in matters of politics and temple administration; the Pharisees were considered scholars and sages held in esteem by ordinary lay folk.

Matthew writes that John strikes a responsive chord in the people who have come to the Jordan River to hear him; but John has strong words for the Pharisees and Sadducees who step up for his baptism but have no intention of embracing the spirit of conversion and renewal to make their own lives ready for the coming of the Messiah. John's confrontation with the Pharisees and Sadducees previews the clash between Jesus and the Jewish leaders that will develop as Matthew's Gospel unfolds.

In proclaiming the Messiah's "baptism in the Holy Spirit and fire," John employs the image of a "winnowing-fan." A winnowing-fan was a flat, wooden, shovel-like tool, used to toss grain into the air. The heavier grain fell to the ground and the chaff was blown away. In the same way, John says, the Messiah will come to gather the "remnant" of Israel while the Godless disappear like dust in the wind.

Every one of us is called in baptism to take on the role of the messenger or prophet (from the Greek word meaning "one who proclaims"). Like the Baptizer in his preaching at the Jordan, the prophet's role is one of bearing witness, with courage, conviction and perseverance, to the presence of God in our own homes and schools and communities and neighborhoods. Our success as prophets is not determined by the number of converts we make, the amount of money we raise for the cause, or the corrupt over-lords and landlords we manage to topple, but in our faithfulness to what is right, what is just, what is of God.

*T*his Christmas, O God,
may we become messengers of your Christ's coming
and prophets of his justice and compassion
  in our midst.
May our gifts of compassion and healing,
our lights of welcome and hope,
our songs of joy and peace proclaim to waiting hearts
that you have come.

Third Sunday of Advent

"Go and tell John what you hear and see: the blind receive their sight, the lame walk, the lepers are cleansed, the deaf hear, the dead are raised, and the poor have the good news brought to them."

Matthew 11: 2–11

Your Christmas gift list

What do you want for Christmas?

Every December, the Santas in our lives ask what gifts we would like to find under the tree on Christmas morning. Then they go to work to make those wishes a reality.

What do you want for Christmas?

Now, the austere John the Baptizer will never be confused for jolly old St. Nick — but John asks us the same question. But John asks us for much more than a wish list of presents. What he asks us is much more profound and urgent.

John asks this Advent: *What are you WANTING FOR this Christmas? What emptiness do you ache to fill? What is missing from your life that God alone can complete?*

John poses the question: *What do you HOPE FOR this Christmas? What would you like this Christmas to be? What would make this Christmas whole, complete, new: A friendship restored? A relationship renewed? A chance to make things right?*

And John challenges us with the most Christmas-like of questions: *What would you GIVE this Christmas? What gifts are you willing to give that can't be wrapped and placed under the tree: Patience? Understanding? Time? What would you be willing to give up in order to make this Christmas special for someone else: your expectation of restitution, your obsession for control, your need to be loved?*

Consider what John asks: *What do you want this Christmas?*

Today's portrait of John is quite different from last Sunday's thundering, charismatic figure preaching to the crowds along the Jordan. John has been imprisoned by Herod for publicly denouncing the king's incestuous marriage to Herodias. John knows that his life is about to end.

This was an anxious time of doubt and despair for John — he had staked his life on proclaiming the long-expected Messiah would come, and his witness will soon cost him his life. John had to wonder if he had been deluding himself. Truth be told, John and the people of Judaism had been expecting a much different kind of Messiah than the gentle, humble Worker of wonders from Nazareth; so John sends friends to ask Jesus if he is, in fact, the Messiah Israel has been waiting for.

Is he the One who will fill our WANTING?

Jesus sends the messengers back to John to report all they have seen Jesus do, fulfilling the prophecies of Isaiah and the prophets of old. Praising John for his faithful witness to the Messiah, Jesus promises his hearers that great things will come to all who become prophets of the reign of God.

The Third Sunday of Advent is sometimes called *Gaudete* Sunday — *Rejoice,* Paul's admonition to the Church at Thessalonica, from which the Entrance Chant for today's liturgy is taken ("Rejoice in the Lord always! I say it again: Rejoice!"). In the midst of the sobering reality that Advent calls us to face, today's Gospel, with its images of the blind seeing, the deaf hearing, the lame walking and the dead being raised to life, gives us cause for hope; the birth of Christ restores our dreams for blooming deserts and flowering wastelands, of hopes restored and brokenness healed. The Christ who comes at Christmas gives us new dreams to work for, new roads to travel to discover the great love and life of God.

The Advent Gospels call us to a much different approach to gift-giving. The most precious gifts we give reflect the God who empties himself of his divinity in order to remake humanity in his holiness; our Christmas giving should mirror the love of God, a love too complete and generous for us to imagine. The true gifts of Christmas that God gives and enables us to give transform the hearts and lives of those we love: gifts of comfort and support, of compassion and reconciliation, of forgiveness and understanding.

*C*ome, Lord, and transform our world
from emptiness to wholeness,
from desert to harvest,
from death to life.
Open eyes that are closed and ears that are deaf
to your presence in our midst;
strengthen those who stumble in their search
  for you;
restore to health those who are mired
  in hurt and despair;
raise up those who are dead to your compassion.

Fourth Sunday of Advent

The angel of the Lord appeared to Joseph in a dream: "Joseph, son of David, do not be afraid to take Mary into your home. For it is through the Holy Spirit that this child has been conceived in her."

Matthew 1: 18–24

The scandal of Emmanuel

*T*he last week of Advent shifts our focus from the promise of the Messiah to the fulfillment of that promise in the events surrounding Jesus' birth.

Today's Gospel is Matthew's version of Jesus' birth. This is not Luke's familiar story of a child born in a Bethlehem stable. Matthew's story is darker; it cannot be romanticized by tinsel or holly or an angelic choir. Matthew writes of a young unmarried woman suddenly finding herself pregnant and her very hurt and confused husband wondering what to do. In Gospel times, marriage was agreed upon by the groom and the bride's parents almost immediately after the age of puberty; but the bride continued to live with her parents after the wedding until the husband was able to support her in his own home or that of his parents. During that interim, marital intercourse was not permitted — but Mary is found to be with child. Joseph, an observant but compassionate Jew, does not wish to subject Mary to the full fury of Jewish law, so he plans to divorce her "quietly."

In Matthew's account, Jesus' coming is a disgrace and a scandal. His birth is a source of humiliation, an embarrassment for his family.

But in images reminiscent of the First Testament "annunciations" of Isaac and Samuel, an angel appears to Joseph in a dream and reveals that this child is the fulfillment of Isaiah's prophecy.

Trusting in God's promise, Joseph acknowledges the child and names him "Jesus" ("God saves") and becomes, in the eyes of the Law, the legal father of Jesus. Thus, Jesus, through Joseph, is born a descendent of David and the fulfillment of Isaiah's prophecy regarding the coming of "Emmanuel" is set into motion.

Despite his own hurt and doubts, despite the scandal and embarrassment, Joseph is asked by God to welcome the Christ child as his own. In Matthew's Gospel, the entire Christ event depends on Joseph, whose life has been turned upside by the angel's news. Joseph puts aside his own confusion and hurt and welcomes the son as his own, not as a matter of biology, but as a matter of love and compassion, of trust and faith. God's birth in our midst depends on human partners — a Mary, a Joseph, a you, a me — willing to believe the impossible, willing to claim the unwanted, willing to love the helpless and neediest, willing to put aside our fears and dare to hope that God is with us. Every one of us is called to be Joseph — to welcome God in our midst. In the mystery of Christmas, God's "yes" depends on our own "yes."

*C*ome, Emmanuel,
and make a dwelling place among us.
May we welcome you into our midst
when your presence is most discomforting,
inconvenient and threatening.
May we give birth to you despite our doubts and fears,
our timidity and weakness.
Come, Emmanuel,
make your dwelling place in our hearts and homes,
despite ourselves.

CHRISTMAS

Christmas: The Nativity of the Lord

And Mary kept all these things, reflecting on them in her heart.

Luke 2: 1–20

Treasures of the heart

*A*s every parent remembers the birth of their son or daughter, Mary, too, remembered. She would often relive those extraordinary days: the discovery of her unexpected pregnancy, her husband's unwavering love and support (despite his confusion and hurt), the excruciating trip to Bethlehem, the terror of that night in the cave, the helplessness and pain of giving birth alone, the appearance of those strange shepherds.

It's a telling detail that Luke includes in his story of Jesus' birth: *Mary kept these things in her heart.* She remembered. She pondered the meaning of what had happened in Nazareth and Bethlehem. Like every mother and father, she would relive every detail of the day of her son's birth and childhood, pondering the question:

What kind of God would do this?

As the rest of the story of her son unfolded, the answer became clearer and clearer:

A God whose love for his creation knows no limits.

A God who loves human beings despite everything and because of everything.

A God who wants human beings to once again breathe divinity, to rejoice in themselves and in one another as sons and daughters of God.

A God of joy, a God of hope, a God of everything that is good.[1]

Christmas invites us, too, to "ponder" these events, to make sense out of the God born this day. Like Mary, we are called to remember the promise of this holy night when God touches human history; like Mary, we are challenged to understand how

---

what God is doing this day reaches out to transform every day; like Mary, we are called to relive the story of Christ as we live out the day-to-day joys and sorrows of our own stories.

Remember this night. Ponder the story. See the hand of God in the details; hear the voice of God narrating the story. Turn down the garish lights and tone down the holiday noise and, in the quiet, behold the Child, behold the mystery, behold the compassion of God that dawned in that cold, cramped, dirty cave.

Consider in your own hearts the mystery:
What kind of God would do this?

The lectionary provides four pericopes of the events that God invites us to "ponder" with Mary this day:

Mass of the Vigil

"Joseph, son of David, do not be afraid to take Mary your wife into your home. For it is through the Holy Spirit that this child has been conceived in her."

Matthew 1: 1–25 [18–25]

*F*or Matthew, the story of Jesus begins with the promise to Abraham — that Jesus is the ultimate and perfect fulfillment of the Law and Prophets. So Matthew begins his Gospel with "a family record" of Jesus, tracing the infant's birth from Abraham (highlighting his Jewish identity) and David (his Messiahship). The accuracy of Matthew's list is dubious; but presenting an historic record is not the evangelist's point. Matthew proclaims in his genealogy that this Jesus is the fulfillment of a world that God envisioned from the first moment of creation — a world created in the justice and peace that is the very nature of its Creator.

Matthew's version of Jesus' birth follows. While Luke's account of Jesus' conception and birth centers around Mary, Joseph is the central figure in Matthew's account. In Matthew's story, Mary is found to be pregnant; her hurt and confused fiancé (who realizes he is not the father) is at a loss as to what to do. Joseph, an observant but compassionate Jew, decides to divorce Mary "quietly" to protect her from the full fury of the Law. But an angel appears to Joseph in a dream and reveals that this child is the fulfillment of Isaiah's prophecy. Putting aside his hurt and placing his trust in God's promise, Joseph acknowledges the child and names him *Jesus* ("Savior") and becomes, in the eyes of the Law, the legal father of Jesus. Because of Joseph's love and compassion for Mary, the Spirit of God sets into motion the dawning of the Christ.

The theme of Matthew's infancy narrative is *Emmanuel* — that Jesus is the promised Christ of old. Isaiah's prophecy has finally been fulfilled in Jesus: the virgin has given birth to a son, one who is a descendent of David's house (through Joseph). Jesus is truly *Emmanuel* — "God is with us."

Mass at Midnight

"For today in the city of David a savior has been born to you who is Christ and Lord."

Luke 2: 1–14

*C*enturies of hope in God's promise have come to fulfillment: the Messiah is born!

Luke's account of Jesus' birth begins by placing the event during the reign of Caesar Augustus. Augustus, who ruled from 27 B.C. until 14 A.D., was honored as "savior" and "god" in ancient Greek inscriptions. His long reign was hailed as the *pax Augusta* — a period of peace throughout the vast Roman world. Luke deliberately points out that it is during the rule of Augustus — the savior, god and peace-maker — that Jesus the Christ, the long-awaited Savior and Messiah, the Son of God and Prince of Peace, enters human history.

Throughout Luke's Gospel, it is the poor, the lowly, the outcast and the rejected who immediately embrace the preaching of Jesus. The announcement of the Messiah's birth to shepherds — who were among the most isolated and despised in the Jewish community — reflects Luke's theme that the poor are the blessed of God.

Mass at Dawn

"Let us go, then, to Bethlehem to see this thing that has taken place which the Lord has made known to us."

Luke 2: 15–20

*T*ypical of Luke's Gospel, it is the shepherds of Bethlehem — among the poorest and most disregarded of Jewish society — who become the first messengers of the Gospel.

From the Christmas story in Luke's Gospel, we have a romantic image of shepherds as gentle, peaceful figures. But that manger scene image is a far cry from the reality: The shepherds of Biblical times were tough, earthy characters who fearlessly used their clubs to defend their flocks from wolves and other wild animals. They had even less patience for the pompous scribes and Pharisees who treated them as second- and third-class citizens, barring these ill-bred rustics from the synagogue and courts.

Yet it was to shepherds that God first revealed the birth of the Messiah. The shepherds' vision on the Bethlehem hillside proclaims to all people of every place and generation that Christ comes for the sake of all of humankind.

The Gospel for the Mass at dawn ends with the touching detail (above): "And Mary kept all things, reflecting on them in her heart."

Mass of the Day

And the Word became flesh and made his dwelling among us ...

John 1: 1–18

*T*he Gospel for Christmas Day is the beautiful Prologue hymn to John's Gospel. With echoes of Genesis 1 ("In the beginning ..," "the light shines on in darkness ..."), the Prologue exalts Christ as the creative Word of God that comes as the new light to illuminate God's re-creation.

In the original Greek text, the phrase "made his dwelling place among us" is more literally translated as "pitched his tent or tabernacle." The image evokes the Exodus memory of the tent pitched by Israelites for the Ark of the Covenant. God sets up the tabernacle of the new covenant in the body of the Child of Bethlehem.

The reading from John reminds us that Christmas is more than the birth of a child; it is the beginning of the Christ event that will transform and re-create human history, a presence that continues to this day and for all time. In this child, the extraordinary love of God has taken our "flesh" and "made his dwelling among us." In his "Word made flesh," God touches us at the very core of our beings, perfectly expressing his constant and unchanging love.

*L*ord God,
with wonder and gratitude we behold the birth
    of your Christ.
May his birth illuminate our dark nights
with the brightness of your love;
may the good news we hear
in our own chaotic and struggling Bethlehems
bring joy and hope to all our mornings;
may the poverty of his birth and life among us
help us to recognize our own poverty;
may his coming to us as one of us inspire us
to lift up one another in the dignity of being
    your sons and daughters.

The Holy Family

When the magi had departed, behold, the angel of the Lord appeared to Joseph in a dream and said, "Rise, take the child and his mother, flee to Egypt, and stay there until I tell you. Herod is going to search for the child to destroy him."

Matthew 2: 13–15, 19–23
[Roman lectionary]

A family decision

*I*n his book, *All Rivers Run to the Sea,* Elie Wiesel recalls a terrible moment confronting his family. World War II was coming to an end, but the deportation of the Jews continued. Elie, who was 15 at the time, his parents and three sisters faced deportation from their village in Hungary to the Nazi concentration camp at Birkenau. Maria, the family's housekeeper who was a Christian, begged the Wiesels to hide in her family's cabin in the mountains. At first, the Wiesels declined, but Maria persisted. The family gathered at the kitchen table for a family meeting: Should they go with Maria or stay and take their chances? The family decided to stay. Elie Wiesel remembers:

"But why?" Maria implored the family, her voice breaking.

"Because," Elie's father replied, "a Jew must never be separated from his community. What happens to everyone else happens to us as well." Elie's mother wondered aloud whether it might not be better "to send the children with Maria." But the children protested: "We're young and strong. The trip won't be as dangerous for us. If anyone should go with Maria, it's you." After a brief discussion, the Wiesels thanked Maria, but ... Elie Wiesel writes of their decision: "My father was right. We wanted to stay together, like everyone else. Family unity is one of our important traditions ... the strength of the family tie, which had contributed to the survival of our people for centuries ... "

The war did not end soon enough for the Wiesels. Only Elie and two of his sisters survived. His mother, father and youngest sister died in the camps.

In addition to the hard life that was the day-to-day lot of Jews in their social and economic class, the family of Joseph, Mary and the child endured a great deal: the scandal of Mary's pregnancy, the difficult and traumatic birth of their child far away from home, the horror of searching for their missing child, and (in today's Gospel) their fleeing for their lives from Herod's murderous wrath. Yet their love for one another and their trust in the Spirit of God in their midst kept this little family together through the worst of times. They survive and persevere, raising their son who grows and develops "in wisdom and age and favor before God and man" (Luke 2: 52).

Matthew's story of Jesus' early years centers on the evangelist's principal theme: that Jesus is the Messiah promised by God long ago. Matthew portrays the Holy Family as outcasts, refugees in their own country. Bound together by love and trust in God and in one another, they embark on the dangerous journey to Egypt to flee the insane rage of Herod. Jesus relives the Exodus experience of Israel: he will come out of Egypt, the land of slavery, to establish a new covenant of liberation for the new Israel.

Every family experiences its share of difficult moments and challenges. Today, on this Sunday after Christmas, we celebrate "family" — that unique nucleus of society that nurtures and supports throughout our journey on earth. Within our families, we experience both the heights of joy and the depths of pain. This Christmas season, may we re-discover that special bond that transforms a household into a family — a family that is a harbor of forgiveness and understanding and a safe place of unconditional love, welcome and acceptance.

*L*oving Father,
keep our family within the embrace
    of your loving providence.
In times of crisis and tension,

bless our families with the hope
    of your consolation and forgiveness;
in times of joy and growth,
bless us with a spirit of thankfulness,
never let us forget that you are Father of us all,
the Giver of all that is good.

In the beginning was the Word, and the Word was with God, and the Word was God ... And the Word became flesh and lived among us, and we have seen his glory, the glory of a father's only son, full of grace and truth.

John 1: 1–18
[Common lectionary — NRSV]

God's arms

*M*any years ago, a pastor stopped by the home of a young woman whose husband had been buried the day before. They had only been married three months when death stalked her husband with pneumonia, and brought him down at last.

In one corner an old white-haired woman sat in a low chair, her face half hidden by her hand; her other hand softly rubbed the shoulder of the young widow — little more than a girl — sitting at her feet.

Suddenly the woman turned almost ferociously on the pastor.

"Where is God?" she demanded. "I've prayed to Him. Where is He? You preached once on the 'Everlasting Arms.' Where are they?"

The minister drew his fingertips lightly down the older woman's arm.

"They are here," he said. "They are round you even now. These are the arms of God."[2]

Christmas celebrates more than a single event, more than just the birth of a child in a Bethlehem cave long ago: Christmas celebrates a presence that continues to this day and for all time. "Emmanuel" — "God is with us."

The Gospel for this first Sunday after Christmas is the prologue to John's Gospel. The evangelist John begins his narrative with this beautiful hymn praising the dawning of God's Christ: "The Word became flesh and made his dwelling among us." In the person of Jesus, God's extraordinary and inexplicable love has taken our human form, has lived our human life in all its joys and sorrows, struggles and complexities. In the dawning of Christ, the sacred is no longer some abstract concept of theological theory; God has descended from the heavens to become one of us in order to show us how we might become like him. The love of God takes on a human face, the Word of God becomes "enfleshed" in the child Christ, enabling us to transform our hearts in that love and re-create our world in that Word of justice and compassion. This child is the very light of God, who inspires hearts and spirits to welcome children as gifts of God, to find joy and completeness in loving our beloved, to care for the poorest and neediest creature as if he or she is Christ himself.

In Christ's birth, God touches human history: hope reigns, justice takes root, peace is possible. The challenge to each one of us is to take on the work of "Emmanuel" — to make God's presence tangible by being his "arms" for the hurting, his "hands" to the needy, his "heart" for the grieving.

*C*hrist Jesus,
you are the Word that set all of creation into motion;
you are the Light that illuminates every human life;
you are the love of God in flesh and blood.
Let your Word echo in our hearts
that we may re-create the world
    in the Father's compassion;
let your light shatter the darkness of sin and alienation;
let your love be the glory we seek,
as we struggle to imitate
your example of humble and grateful service
    to one another.

January 1

Mary, the Mother of God
[Roman lectionary]

The Holy Name of Jesus
[Common lectionary]

The shepherds made known the message that had been told them about this child. All who heard it were amazed by what had been told them by the shepherds. And Mary kept all these things, reflecting on them in her heart. When eight days were completed for his circumcision, he was named Jesus ...

Luke 2: 16–21

Let's hear it for the child

This Christmas season, give your children something special. Tell them about the day they were born.

Most children don't come into the world celebrated by angelic hosts and great stars in the sky. But the beginning of each ordinary life is still a once-and-for-all extraordinary event. Telling those stories is a way to tell children just how special they are in our lives and in God's creation — and to give them important clues about themselves.

Tell them about the joy of the day they were born. Tell them any of the crazy stories, the unexpected and surprising details, the special and funny roles of other family members and friends, the painful and anxious moments that are part of their entrance into human history.

Tell them of your odyssey in arranging for their adoption. Say to them: *You are so important to us that we were willing to go to such great pains to bring you into our lives.*

Tell them the details of their nativity, their Christmas.

And when you tell them their story, remind them how glad you are that they came into your life, that the love in which they were conceived and welcomed, is still very much present.[3]

In the birth of the Christ Child, the love of God has become real to us — and remains real to us in our own births and lives and those of our children. Christ's birth is our birth, too, as a people reborn in God's love. God transforms our lives by taking on our humanity, becoming of us and with us in all of life's complications and complexities, triumphs and tragedies, delights and depressions. In the birth of Christ, as in the births of those we love, God calls us to embrace the hope and potential of this life and to realize what an extraordinary gift is this life that God has breathed into us.

On the threshold of a new calendar year, the Gospels for January 1 invite us, as does Mary in the midst of all that has happened in Bethlehem, to "reflect" in our own hearts what has taken place in the birth of this Child.

In the Roman Catholic tradition, today's solemnity honors Mary under her most ancient title — *Theotokos,* "Bearer of God": In accepting her role as mother of the Messiah, she becomes the first disciple of her Son, the first to embrace his Gospel of hope, compassion and reconciliation. As Mary, the young unmarried pregnant girl, believes and trusts in the incredible thing that she is to be a part of, even the most ordinary of us can believe in our parts in the drama, too.

In other traditions, January 1 honors the Holy Name of Jesus. Today's liturgy centers on the Gospel account of Jesus' circumcision at which he is given the name that not only identifies him but also marks the life he will live for the sake of humanity. It is the name we take on in our baptismal commitment to live the life of his Gospel. By his name, we are called to "give birth" to God in the stables and barns of our own time and place. "The Lord saves" in every work of compassion and mercy we extend, in the peace and justice we struggle to bring to our own Bethlehems and Nazareths and Jerusalems.

*F*ather of compassion,
in baptism we are reborn in the life of your Son;
we take on his name:
Jesus, "The Lord saves";
Christ, "the anointed of God."
May we live that name every day of this New Year:
may we create a dwelling place for you
in our works of charity and reconciliation;
may we give birth to you
in every word of consolation and support we speak,
in every joy we bring into the lives of others.

Epiphany

Magi from the east arrived in Jerusalem, saying, "Where is the newborn king of the Jews? We saw his star at its rising and have come to do him homage."

Matthew 2: 1–12

Traveling by star

In December 1954, Carlo Carretto abandoned his life as a successful teacher and renowned writer and activist in Italy and set out for the Algerian Sahara to become a Little Brother of Jesus. He wrote about his ten-year pilgrimage in the African desert in his book *Letters from the Desert.*

"The first nights I spent here made me send off for books on astronomy and maps of the sky; and for months afterwards I spent my free time learning a little of what was passing over my head up there in the universe ... kneeling on the sand, I sank my eyes for hours and hours at those wonders, writing down my discoveries in an exercise book like a child ... "

"Finding one's way in the desert is much easier by night than by day ... In the years which I spent in the open desert I never once got lost, thanks to the stars. Many times ... I lost my way because the sun was too high in the sky. But I waited for night and found the road again, guided by the stars.

"How dear they were to me, those stars: how close to them the desert had brought me. Through spending my nights in the open, I had come to know them by their names, then to study them, and to get to know them one by one. Now I could distinguish their color, their size, their position, their beauty. I knew my way around them, and from them I could calculate the time without a watch."[4]

Like Carlo Carretto and his brothers in the desert, like the astrologers of the Epiphany story, we are all star watchers and star gazers. What and who we read and watch and listen to in search of wealth, fame and power are the stars we follow — but the magi and Brother Carlo set their sights on a different star that leads them to God. Their sightings set them off on journeys of faith, journeys of discovery at the wonder of this gift of life and the Giver of life.

The story of the magi's search for the newborn Christ is not a romantic tale with a happy ending. Their journey, guided by the star in the desert sky, is the beginning of a story of suffering and hardship and death; it is the prelude to a lifelong struggle to bring justice to a place broken by conflict, to heal a people scarred by war and hatred. Yet the Gospel of God's Christ is a story of hope amid the bloodshed, of life conquering death, of love rising from the ashes.

The story of the astrologers and the star of Bethlehem is unique to Matthew's Gospel. Note that Matthew does not call them kings nor does he give their names nor reports where they came from — in fact, Matthew never even specifies the number of magi (because three gifts are presented to the Child, it has been a tradition since the fifth century to picture "three wise men"). In stripping away the romantic layers that have been added to the story over the centuries, Matthew's point becomes clearer.

A great many Old Testament ideas and images are presented in this story of *epiphany* (from the Greek word for *appearance* or *manifestation).* The star, for example, is reminiscent of Balaam's prophecy that "a star shall advance from Jacob" (Numbers 24: 17). Many of the details in Matthew's story about the child Jesus parallel the story of the child Moses and the Exodus.

Most importantly, Matthew's story provides a preview of what is to come. First, the reactions of the various parties to the birth of Jesus parallel the effects Jesus' teaching will have on those who hear it. Herod reacts with anger and hostility to the Jesus of the poor who comes to overturn the powerful and rich. The chief priests and scribes greet the news with haughty indifference toward the Jesus who comes to give new life and meaning to the rituals and laws of the scribes. But the magi — non-believers in the eyes of Israel — possess the humility of faith and the openness of mind and heart to seek and welcome the Jesus who will institute the Second Covenant between God and the New Israel.

The gifts of the astrologers indicate the principal dimensions of Jesus' mission:

- **gold** is a gift worthy for a king, a ruler, one with power and authority;
- **frankincense** is an appropriate gift for a priest, one who offers sacrifice (frankincense was an aromatic perfume sprinkled on the animals sacrificed in the Temple);
- **myrrh** is a "gift" for someone whose death is imminent (myrrh was used in ancient times for embalming the bodies of the dead before burial).

We all travel through life guided by stars, stars of various degrees of illumination. The Epiphany challenges us set our sights on the "star" of God that leads us to the joy and lasting treasures of "Emmanuel", God present in every step and turn of our journey.

*C*hrist, the very light of God,
be the star we follow on our journey
    to the dwelling place of God;
in your light, may we recognize all men and women
as our brothers and sisters under the loving providence
    of the Father of all.
Illuminate the roads and paths we travel,
that we may not stumble or turn back
from your way of peace, forgiveness and justice.

Baptism of the Lord

After Jesus was baptized ... a voice came from the heavens, saying, "This is my beloved Son, with whom I am well pleased."

Matthew 3: 13–17

Welcome to the sandbox

*M*ikey is having a bad day — as bad a day as a six-year-old can have. There was the paint he knocked over while running in his classroom, the punch he threw at his little sister who kept bugging him while he was playing on the computer, and the meatloaf sandwich for lunch that he wanted no part of and made his position unmistakably clear. And now, on this particular afternoon, there was nobody around to play with. So Mikey found himself exiled to the sandbox, mindlessly pushing his prized toy dump truck through the dirt.

After a while, he saw his dad come around the corner. Mom must have filled him in on the day's misadventures. Mikey didn't look up, he didn't say a word. He just kept pushing his truck through the sand — and steeled himself for the worst.

When Dad got to the edge of the sandbox, he squatted and sat next to Mikey. Dad said nothing as he took a pail, filled it with sand, and carefully turned it over at one end of the rut Mikey had cut through the sand. Dad then made another perfect mound of sand, and then another. Mikey smiled for the first time all day. And for the next half hour or so, Mikey and his dad transformed the sandbox into an elaborate network of roads and bridges.

In today's Gospel, Jesus begins his public ministry by getting in line and waiting his turn to be baptized by John. Like Mikey's dad, he gets into the "sandbox" with us. In him, Emmanuel — "God-is-with-us" — meant God being in the river with us, in the flesh with us, in the joys and sorrows, in the discoveries and quandaries that are part of everyone's life.

Jesus' baptism at the Jordan River by John is the final piece of the Epiphany. The Baptizer's refusal at first to baptize Jesus and Jesus' insistence (a dialogue that appears only in Matthew's Gospel) speaks to Matthew's continuing theme of Jesus as the fulfillment of the First Testament prophecies. Jesus clearly did not need to be baptized. But his baptism by John is an affirmation that God was with this Jesus in a very special way – at the Jordan River, Isaiah's prophecy is fulfilled: "my favor rests on him." Jesus has come to identify with sinners, to bring them forgiveness, to heal them of their brokenness and mend their relationship with God — hence the propriety of Jesus' acceptance of John's baptism.

Baptism was a ritual performed by the Jews, usually for those who entered Judaism from another religion. It was natural that the sin-stained, polluted pagan should be "washed" in baptism, but no Jew could conceive of needing baptism, being born a son of Abraham, one of God's chosen people and therefore assured of God's salvation. But John's baptism — a baptism affirmed by Jesus — was not one of initiation, but one of reformation, a rejection of sin in one's own life and acknowledgment of one's own need for conversion. In Christ, baptism becomes a sacrament of rebirth, the reception of new life.

In all the Gospel accounts of Jesus' baptism, all four evangelists use a similar description of the scene at the Jordan: The Spirit of God descended and rested upon Jesus, "hovering" over him like a dove. As the Gospel story unfolds, the Spirit of God's peace, compassion and love, will be the constant presence dwelling within and flowing forth from the Carpenter from Nazareth. In our own baptisms, we embrace that same Spirit that now "hovers" over us, guiding us in our journey to God.

Jesus comes to enter our sandboxes in all of our "Mikey" moments. The mystery of the Epiphany sequence is not what God gives up but what he takes on: *us*. He shows us that we are not just the subject of his work, we *are* his work; that we will be not just witnesses of his glory, we *are* his glory. In Christ, we are all in the river and the sandbox together; with Christ, we can transform our lives from darkness to light, we can re-create our world from sinful selfishness to hope-filled community.

Raise us up out of the waters of our baptism, O God,
and send down your Spirit to dwell within our hearts.
May we live lives of humble gratitude and integrity,
    always aware that your love is a power
    greater than anything we possess of our own;
may our struggle to live faithfully the Gospel
    of your beloved Son
make us worthy of our baptismal Christian name.
May your presence in our midst
transform our homes and hearts
into the dwelling place of your compassion and mercy.

LENT

Ash Wednesday

"Your Father who sees what is hidden will repay you."
Matthew 6: 1–6, 16–18

Even now, says the Lord, return to me with your whole heart …
Joel 2: 12–18

We implore you, in Christ's name, be reconciled to God.
2 Corinthians 5: 20 – 6:2

"Simple gifts"

*L*isten to the words of the wonderful Shaker hymn, *Simple Gifts*. Listen — with a Lenten ear:

> *'Tis the gift to be simple, 'tis the gift to be free,*
> *'Tis the gift to come down where you ought to be,*
> *And when we find ourselves in the place just right,*
> *'Twill be in the valley of love and delight.*
> *When true simplicity is gained,*
> *To bow and to bend we shan't be ashamed;*
> *To turn, turn will be our delight,*
> *'Til by turning, turning we come round right.*

During the Lenten season we begin today, the Spirit of God calls us to live and seek the two major themes of this wonderful old hymn.

Lent calls us, first, to recapture holy *simplicity:* to put aside the many things that complicate our lives and to focus again on the simple but profound things of God — love, joy, compassion, forgiveness, justice. These next 40 days call us to free ourselves of the empty and shallow values that take over our lives and become the people we truly want to be in the eyes of God.

This is also the season of *turning.* The words repentance (Hebrew) and conversion (Latin) come from the same root: *to turn.* Lent (from the Anglo-Saxon word for *spring)* is the season for *turning:* The earth completes its spring "turning" toward the sun; we soon begin the "turning" of the ground for the spring planting. As the prophet Joel proclaims in today's first reading, this is the time for a "turning" of our hearts and spirits in the Shaker spirit of *turning* — turning away from those things that diminish us and that steal our time and energy away from those we love and turning toward the things of God.

The three readings for Ash Wednesday all call us to a *turning* of perspective and attitude:

In today's Gospel, from his Sermon on the Mount, Jesus instructs his listeners on the Christian attitude and disposition toward prayer, fasting and almsgiving. Such acts are meaningful only if they are outward manifestations of the essential *turning* that has taken place within our hearts.

The prophet Joel, in today's first reading, calls the people of Judah to repent, to *turn* to the Lord with fasting, prayer and works of charity. A devastating invasion of locusts has ravaged Judah (around 400 BC). The prophet sees this catastrophe as a sign of the coming "Day of the Lord" and pleads with the community to turn away from their self-absorbed lives and re-turn to the God of mercy and graciousness.

The Church at Corinth is a deeply divided community. Some factions have challenged Paul himself and his mandate as an apostle. In his second letter to the Corinthians (today's second reading), Paul alternates between anger and compassion, between frustration and affection, in appealing for reconciliation and unity — for a re-*turn* to the one faith they all share as the Church of the Risen Christ.

This is the season for the hard but never fully completed work of conversion — the everyday struggle of *turning* to embrace the life and love of God until we arrive, in the end, "in the place just right ... the valley of love and delight."

*C*hrist Jesus,
be with us on the Lenten journey we begin today.
Teach us the way of holy simplicity,
that with joy and humility
we may put aside whatever distracts us
from your love and grace.
Turn us —
turn us away from the cold darkness
of self-centeredness and fear,
turn us toward the radiant light of Easter resurrection.

After being baptized, Jesus was led by the Spirit into the desert to be tempted by the devil.

Matthew 4: 1–11

Wilderness experiences

*I*n a cost-cutting move, corporate eliminated his position. In his mid 40s, he knew that other companies would hardly be lining up to hire him. He learned about a support group for professional, technical and managerial job seekers. The group helped him work through the shock, disbelief, resentment and anger experienced by anyone who loses a job; the volunteer counselors worked with him to rebuild both his skills and self-esteem and focus on what he wanted to do next in his life. His "desert experience" between jobs was a time of discovery and growth from confusion to clarity, from resentment to humility, from a sense of failure to hope.

After 15 years of marriage, she was suddenly a widow. Theirs was a warm and loving marriage — each was the other's protector, confidant and best friend. The weeks after his death were a fog of grief and heartbreaking loneliness. Slowly, she started to work through the tangle of legal and financial details. With the help of family and friends, she began to put her life back together. These were difficult, painful days, but from this "desert sojourn" she moved on to the next chapter of her life.

For most high school seniors, applying to college is the first big decision of their young lives. Pages of applications must be written and submitted, financial aid forms must be completed, SATs must be prepared for and taken, visits must be arranged to the various campuses. Then it becomes a time of waiting — waiting for the test results, waiting for that fat packet with the letter of acceptance, waiting for the financial aid availability. And while waiting, there is also self-doubt and second-guessing: *Am I really ready for this? What do*

I want out of the next four years? What do I want to do with my life after college? For every high school senior, the college application process is a "desert experience" from childhood to adulthood.

We experience many "wilderness experiences" throughout our lives — times of change, decision, transition, growth, and discovery. Jesus begins his public ministry with just such a period of discernment as to what exactly God was calling him to do and be in this next and climactic period of his life.

In Matthew's account of Jesus' forty-day desert experience, Jesus is confronted with several choices. All of the tempter's offers would have Jesus sin against the great commandment of Deuteronomy: "You shall love the Lord your God with all your heart, and with all your soul, and with all your strength." (Deuteronomy 6:5) The tempter offers comfort, wealth and power, but Jesus chooses, instead, the course of humble and prayerful servanthood that the Father has chosen for him. All of Jesus' responses to the devil's challenges are found in Deuteronomy (8:3, 6: 16, 6:13).

The same Spirit that led Jesus into the desert accompanies us in our desert experiences of grief, loss, despair, fear, and struggle. Every moment of our lives demands that we make hard choices, choices that challenge us either to live the values we believe in the depths of our hearts or forsake those values for things of far less worth or permanence. The season of Lent calls us to embrace God's Spirit of truth so that we may make the choices demanded by our complicated and complex world with courage, insight and faith.

O God, lead us this Lent into the deserts of our hearts.
Let these days be a time
of discernment and discovery,
of resolution and conversion.
May your Word be our bread
    during our wilderness journey;
may your light illuminate the treacherous turns
    of the road we walk;
may your grace and wisdom minister to us
    in our deserts of sadness and despair.

Second Sunday of Lent

Jesus was transfigured before Peter, James and John; his face shone like the sun and his clothes became white as light ... From the cloud came a voice that said:
"This is my beloved Son with whom I am well pleased; listen to him."

Matthew 17: 1–9
[Roman lectionary]

Light within

A young husband and wife learn they are about to become parents for the first time. They are excited, of course — but there is a lingering doubt: *How can I be a parent to a child when I'm still pretty much a kid myself? Do I have what it takes to be a good mom, a good dad? I mean, I could really destroy a great kid here!* But the young parents find within themselves the wisdom, the strength, the patience — the grace — to be a good mom and dad to this child whom they love more than they could ever imagine.

She took care of every detail of their family's life together. Then she became ill — and suddenly it was now all up to him. At first, he was lost, terrified. But he managed to make it all work: to handle the demands of the household, to keep everyone on schedule, to be dad and sometimes mom to the kids — all the while continuing to be a strong and supportive husband to her. With the help of family and friends — and her — he found within himself the patience and where-with-all to keep family and home together.

Every life is a continuing series of such self-discoveries:

A boy picks up a bat for the first time. A girl takes her first tentative steps onto the court and begins dribbling the basketball.

He nervously steps up to the lectern and clears his throat. She stares at the blank page for a long time before she begins writing down words — her words.

He bends down to help, not knowing what he should do. She sits by the bedside, having no idea what to say.

Who are we to think we can play this game, succeed at this craft, express anything important in art, offer any meaningful support or consolation (terrified, in fact, that we are certain to say the wrong thing or do something to make things worse)?

But when we confront our fears, when we resolve to give all we have, when we devote the time to learn and practice, we amaze ourselves at the talents and abilities we possess and what we can do.

In our lives, we confront many mountains: the first day at a new school, new responsibilities at work, a desperate call for help. But we manage to find within ourselves abilities we didn't know we possessed, words we didn't think we knew, love that was beyond us. We realize in those moments that we are, in fact, smart enough, capable enough, loving enough to learn, to succeed, to heal, to transform our lives and the world around us.

Those moments of discovering what we are able to do and our willingness to take on new responsibilities as a result are moments of "transfiguration." Matthew's use of the Greek word *transfigured* indicates that what the disciples saw in Jesus on Mount Tabor was a divinity that shone from within him. Matthew's account of that extraordinary scene (which Matthew places six days after Jesus' first prediction of his passion and his first instructions on the call to discipleship) is filled with images from the First Testament: the voice which repeats Isaiah's "Servant" proclamation, the appearance of Moses and Elijah, the dazzling white garments of Jesus. Peter and his companions are too stunned to realize the full meaning of what they are seeing — that will come when they descend the mountain with Jesus and complete the journey to Jerusalem.

What Peter, James and John see in Jesus is his divinity, the very life of God in Jesus. A spark of that same divinity exists within each one of us, as well: The compassion of God is present within us, animating us to do things we can't imagine doing, guiding our steps as we try to walk justly and humbly in the ways of God, enlightening our vision with wisdom and selflessness to bring the justice and mercy of God to our world. The challenge of discipleship is to allow the love of God within us to "trans-figure" despair into hope, sadness into joy, anguish into healing, estrangement into community.

O Christ, the very Light and Word of God,
may this Lent be an experience of transfiguration for us.
Illuminate our spirits
that we may rediscover the sense of the sacred
    within ourselves.
May that sacredness enable us to see
beyond our own needs, wants and interests
so that we may set about to transfigure
    our lives and our world
in your compassion, justice and forgiveness.

[In the Common Lectionary, this Gospel
is read on the Last Sunday after Epiphany —
the Sunday before Ash Wednesday.]

Jesus' encounter with Nicodemus: "God did not send the Son into the world to condemn the world, but in order that the world might be saved through him."

John 3: 1–17
[Common lectionary]

Patron saint of seekers

*T*oday's Gospel is one of three appearances of the Pharisee Nicodemus in John's Gospel.

Nicodemus, as a Pharisee and teacher, was a member of the Jewish ruling class. He is described as one of a small group of Jewish elite who are favorably disposed to Jesus, but do not totally understand him nor his teachings. Intrigued by Jesus but not wanting to raise suspicions, Nicodemus comes to Jesus in the middle of the night (in John's Gospel, night and darkness symbolize doubt or lack of faith). For the evangelist John, Nicodemus represents exactly the kind of timid disciple the evangelist seeks to persuade to come forward and openly profess his/her faith in Jesus as the Christ.

In the dialogue that follows, Jesus explains that the kingdom of God he proclaims is not the geographic or political entity Israel has longed for; the reign of God he has come to establish is a state of being that transcends time and place. To enter the realm of God demands an interior transformation in the Spirit (in the original Greek, Jesus' words in verse 3 can be translated either as one must be "born from above" or that one be "born again.") Invoking the image of Moses' staff of a bronze serpent raised to save the Israelites from the bite of poisonous snakes (Numbers 21:9), Jesus prophesies his own death, when he will be "lifted up" for the glory of God and the salvation of humankind. And, in arguably the most famous verse in John's Gospel, Jesus speaks of a God who is motivated by love so great that the Father has given the world his own Son not to condemn but to save.

Nicodemus will appear later in John's Gospel (John 7: 50–52), when a plot to do away with Jesus is taking shape. In the course of the debate, Nicodemus will defend Jesus, arguing that it is against the holy law to condemn anyone before a hearing; Nicodemus will be ridiculed by the council for his position. On Good Friday, Nicodemus will appear at the foot of the cross, bringing myrrh and aloes to assist Joseph of Arimathea — another follower of Jesus, like Nicodemus, "a secret one for fear of the Jews" — to prepare Jesus' body for hasty burial (John 19: 38–40).

Nicodemus is often portrayed as a coward, skulking around Jesus at night or when Jesus is dead, always playing it safe, avoiding commitments and entanglements that might place him on the "wrong" side. His training as a Pharisee has limited his faith to a narrow, literal interpretation of his religion and its law. But despite our derision of Nicodemus, Jesus welcomes him as a sincere seeker of God. Jesus senses that his words have struck a nerve in Nicodemus, that Nicodemus is wrestling with Jesus' more liberating and complete wisdom that is well beyond Nicodemus' comfort zone.

We are like Nicodemus. We struggle to make sense of Jesus; we wrestle with trying to reconcile his Gospel with the demands of our world. But Jesus neither rejects us nor ridicules us but walks with us in our doubts and indecision, our moving back and forth between what is safe and familiar and the new but demanding love of God.

While we tend to see God as the great cosmic Ruler, a mysterious Being totally detached from us and removed from the human experience, Jesus reveals God as a loving Father who created us and our world out of love and seeks to restore his beloved creation through an even greater act of love — God's becoming human himself in order that his beloved humanity might realize God's dream of becoming holy and sacred.

To be "born in the Spirit" is to see things with the eyes of God, to honor what God honors, to love as God loves us. The kingdom of God that Jesus speaks of in the Gospel transcends boundaries and labels, stereotypes and traditions, the color of flags and the color of skin. In God's eyes, we are all his children; in God's heart, we are all brothers and sisters to one another.

Each one of us is a seeker like Nicodemus, trying to make our way from the darkness of doubt and confusion and into the light of wisdom and truth. God, the Author of love, sends his Beloved to walk with us and show us the way out of our darkest nights and into the morning of eternity.

*C*hrist Jesus,
may we born anew in the water of the life of the Father
and the Spirit of compassion and peace.
Open our hearts and consciences to embrace your Gospel
despite our doubts and fears.
Be our courage and strength
as we cope with the obstacles of our lives
that remove us and isolate us from you.
Walk with us as we struggle to become your disciples
and live lives worthy of our identity
    as sons and daughters of the Father
and brothers and sisters to one another in you.

Jesus meets the Samaritan woman at Jacob's well: " ... whoever drinks the water I shall give will never thirst; the water I shall give will become in him a spring of water welling up to eternal life."

John 4: 5–42

Water, the sage and teacher

A great teacher of the East was renowned for his wisdom and insight. People would travel great distances to meet and talk with him. He was most generous in sharing what he had discerned from his many years of prayer, study and discernment.

One of his students asked him who had been his greatest teacher.

The old sage's surprising response: Water.

Water, he explained, is yielding but all-conquering. Water extinguishes fire, or, finding itself defeated by flame, escapes as steam and then re-forms as Water. Water washes away soft Earth, or, when confronted by Rock, seeks a way around it. Water corrodes Iron till it crumbles to dust; it saturates the atmosphere so that Wind dies. Water gives way to obstacles with deceptive humility, for no power can prevent it following its destined course to the sea. Water conquers by yielding; it never attacks but always wins the last battle.

The wise teacher said to the student that whoever makes himself like Water is distinguished for his humility; the student of Water embraces the power of righteousness and the way of peace; the disciple of Water acts from a place of thoughtful stillness and conquers the world.

Water is the predominant image in today's readings: As water sustains life and cleans away the grime and filth that can diminish and destroy life, the waters of baptism wash away the sins that alienate us from God so that we are reborn in the Spirit of compassion and community. Today's Gospel has long had a special place in baptismal catechesis: In revealing himself as the Messiah to the Samaritan woman, Jesus speaks of himself as "life-giving water ... a fountain welling up [within you] to eternal life." From Jacob's well springs forth the living waters of the Messiah Christ.

Jesus' meeting the Samaritan woman at Jacob's well mirrors the principal role of Jesus as the Messiah: to reconcile all men and women to the Father. As a Samaritan, the woman is considered an outcast by the Jews; as a known adulteress, she is scorned by her own village. With kindness and dignity, Jesus reconciles her to God. The Samaritan woman is, for the evangelist John, a model of a disciple's experience of faith: In her personal encounter with Jesus, she confronts her own sinfulness and need for forgiveness; she then comes to realize the depth of God's love for her; reconciled with God, her life is transformed; she is then sent forth to share with others what she has seen and heard of this Jesus.

Water is the great teacher for those who would be a disciple of Jesus: humble in service to others and giving one's self totally and completely to nurture and sustain the tiniest spark of life, the disciple of Jesus ultimately triumphs in the certainty of the reign of God. From the "water" that is Christ, we satisfy our thirst for meaning and purpose, for hope and resurrection — and we then become that water for those thirsting for those same things and for a world parched by strife and division and drained of compassion and justice.

*C*hrist Jesus, you are the living water of God:
Satisfy our thirst for justice and peace in our lives,
bring life to the barren stretches
    of isolation and despair in our lives.

Christ Jesus, you are the anointed one of God:
Show us the way to the Father that passes through
    every human heart.

Christ Jesus, you are the light of God:
Open our hearts and spirits to see ourselves
    as Samaritans
who have experienced your healing and forgiveness
and whom you now call to bring
your healing and forgiveness to others.

The healing of the man born blind: "Rabbi, who sinned, this man or his parents, that he was born blind?"

"Neither he nor his parents sinned; it is so that the works of God might be made visible through him …

"I came into this world for judgment, so that those who do not see might see, and those who do see might become blind."

John 9: 1–41

Angela's parents

After the anticipation and anxiety experienced by all parents-to-be (especially first-time parents), a couple rejoices in the birth of their first child. They name her Angela — "the angel, the messenger." But it is soon apparent that something is not right. Angela is found to have Down's syndrome. Angela's parents are shocked, hurt, disappointed, and angry that this could happen to *their* daughter.

But a mother and father's love can overcome a great deal. Angela is and always will be their beautiful baby daughter. They find within themselves wells of patience and love they never imagined they possessed. They study everything they can about their daughter's condition and become advocates on her behalf and for other children with Down's syndrome. They make themselves available to counsel other parents and families coping with the same situation. With her parents' love and support, Angela grows up and lives a happy, fulfilled life and inspires others like her to do the same.

In Angela and her family, "the works of God are made visible … "

In their compassion and generosity of spirit, Angela's parents have embraced the vision that is the theme of today's Gospel. They have managed to put aside their own hurt and bitterness to become loving parents to their daughter — and more: They become an inspiration and an example of hope to other parents and families facing the same situation. They become the very light that illuminated their own hard journey dealing with the reality of their daughter's illness.

As was water in last week's Gospel, light is the unifying image in John's account of Jesus' curing the man born blind. Jesus calls himself "the light of the world" who comes to "smear" our own eyes in order to see the hand of God at work in all things; he is the light that illuminates new paths, new perspectives, new angles on old truths, new colors and textures.

While his synoptic counterparts recount Jesus' miracles as manifestations of his great love and compassion, John "stages" Jesus' miracles in order to reveal the deeper meanings of Jesus' mission of redemption as the Messiah. His story of the healing of the man born blind is really a play with six scenes: the blind beggar's healing with the mud that Jesus mixes on the Sabbath; the people's reaction to his cure; the beggar's testimony before the Pharisees; the testimony of the blind man's parents; the beggar's second appearance before the Pharisees (resulting in his expulsion); the beggar's return to Jesus and Jesus' confrontation with the Pharisees.

The "play" begins with Jesus challenging the prevailing belief that serious illness or catastrophe is a sign of God's displeasure with the individual — bad things only happened to bad people. To the question who was to blame for the tragedy of the man born blind, Jesus replies *Nobody*. The young man's blindness will become a means for revealing God's compassion in their midst. Jesus also refuses to countenance the assigning of blame as a coping mechanism. He challenges his disciples to discern the light of God in the midst of the prevailing darkness. Even the greatest tragedy can become an occasion of grace if we seek resurrection rather than recrimination.

The healing of the man born blind heightens the tension between Jesus and the Pharisees. The teaching of this itinerant Rabbi threatens the structured and exalted life of the scribes and Pharisees. They seek to discredit Jesus any way they can — and this "miracle" gives them the opportunity. In using spittle to knead clay and then rubbing it on the man's eyes, Jesus breaks the strict rules prohibiting any kind of manual labor on the Sabbath. The miracle itself becomes secondary; the issue becomes Jesus' profaning the Sabbath. At this point in John's Gospel, the Pharisees are so embittered against Jesus that they are prepared to do anything — even manipulate ecclesiastical procedures — to destroy Jesus. Jesus' "work" of compassion on the Sabbath is a direct challenge to the emptiness, the coldness of their scrupulous following of the Law.

The real "blindness" in this encounter is suffered by those whose who cannot see the goodness of God in their midst, who fail to recognize the sin in their own lives, who do not realize the absence of compassion and forgiveness in their lives. In the course of this Gospel, the blind man and the Pharisees move in opposite directions: the man moves toward the light of faith and understanding, while the Pharisees plunge into the darkness of willful ignorance and isolation from the life and love of God.

(The inquisition of the blind man and his parents — scenes three and four — and his expulsion from the temple — scene five — are important parts of the story for the evangelist and his readers. John and his community of Jewish-Christians are experiencing the same rejection, many of them having been expelled from their synagogues and the temple for their belief in Jesus as the Messiah.)

For the blind man and his parents in today's Gospel, the love of God becomes real to them in the compassion of Jesus; for Angela and her parents, grief is transformed into blessing, disappointment is transformed into gratitude, when they rediscover the light of God's love illuminating their lives.

*C*hrist our light,
open our eyes to see the possibilities
for hope in the midst of despair,
for healing the most painful and traumatic wounds,
for reconciliation despite the deepest chasms
    of mistrust and hatred.
May we then become for others
the light of your compassion and peace
that has illuminated and re-created our hearts.

Jesus cried out in a loud voice, "Lazarus, come out!"
The dead man came out, tied hand and foot with burial bands,
and his face wrapped in a cloth.
"Untie him and let him go."

John 11: 1–45

Our little boxes

*T*he bulletin item asks for volunteers for a soup kitchen or clothing drive. That group does so many good things for the poor and needy and we know it would be a wonderful experience to be a part of it. But we're afraid we might become too committed, afraid of actually meeting and getting to know poor people (as if we could somehow "catch" their poverty), afraid of the surprised reactions of friends over our sudden "do-good-ism." So we stay in our own comfortable little *box*.

Someone we know has been diagnosed with a serious illness, or they have lost a job, or their son or daughter has gotten into trouble. We'd like to call; we'd like to offer to help. But we don't really know what to say or do or offer. We are concerned that we will say the wrong thing and make matters worse. Besides, we reason, there are people a lot closer to them who can help better than we can. Better for all concerned that we not venture too far out of our safe little *box*.

The promotion is within sight; the raise is all but ours. Nobody and nothing will stand in our way. If it means so many nights and weekends away from the family, no problem; compromise a few scruples, so be it; swallow some minor injustices, that's to be expected. After all, we all have to pay the mortgage on our little *box*.

The "boxes" we create for ourselves can quickly become "tombs" in which our hope, our yearning to love and be loved, our dreams of forgiveness and reconciliation disintegrate and die. Every one of us is caught up in some obsession, some distraction, some behavior that prevents us from being the kind of spouse, parent, child or friend that we want to be. We can let our anger, disappointment, cynicism and despair bind us up and bury us in tombs we cannot extricate ourselves from. The Lenten journey calls us to confront such sin before we become totally "dead" to the life that exists around us. Jesus calls not only to Lazarus but to all of us: *Come out! Go free! Unbind yourselves from the wrappings of death!*

As was the case in John's account of the healing of the man born blind (last Sunday's Gospel), the raising of Lazarus is more than just a sign of Jesus' love and compassion. Each of the seven miracles that John includes in his Gospel ("the Book of Signs," as this section of John's Gospel is titled) is dramatized by the evangelist to underscore some dimension of the redemptive nature of Jesus' work. Today's Gospel, the climactic sign in John's Gospel, plays like a rehearsal for the events that next week's liturgies will celebrate. Lazarus' experience prefigures the life that Jesus, the "resurrection and the life" (who will, ironically, be put to death because, in part, of his gift of life to Lazarus), will give to all who believe in him once he has been raised from the dead. The Christ who consoles Martha and Mary consoles us with the promise that death is not an end but a beginning; the Christ who raises Lazarus from his grave calls us out of the graves of bitterness and anger we dig for ourselves and to walk together in the light and promise of his resurrection; the Christ who unties Lazarus' burial cloths and wrappings frees us from the fear and despair that bind us from experiencing the love of God to its fullness.

Raise us out of the tombs we have dug for ourselves,
O Lord,
that we may experience the life of God to the fullest.
Put your hand to ours to roll away the stones
that seal us off from the love of family and friends;
Untie our hands and feet from the bindings of death
so that we may walk with courage and hope
to the kingdom of our Father;
remove the veils from our faces
so that we may see you in the faces of one another.

Sunday of the Lord's Passion: Palm Sunday

The Blessing and Procession of Palms

The disciples brought the ass and colt and laid their coats upon them, and Jesus sat upon them. The very large crowd spread their cloaks on the road, while others cut branches from the trees and strewed them on the road.

Matthew 21: 1–11

The blessed colt

*I*n his story of Jesus' Palm Sunday entry into Jerusalem, the evangelist Matthew seems to make the donkey and colt the center of the story. Matthew relates with surprising detail how the disciples found the animals as Jesus told them. As Jesus intended, they are important players in the Palm Sunday Gospel.

Matthew's account of Jesus' entry into the city of Jerusalem is framed by the prophecy of Zechariah (9:9). It was the custom for pilgrims to enter Jerusalem on foot. Only great kings and rulers would "ride" into the city — and usually on great steeds. Jesus, the King of the new Jerusalem, chooses to ride into the city — but not on a majestic stallion but on the back of a young beast of burden. By being led through the city on the back of a lowly, servile donkey, Jesus comes as a King whose rule is not about being served but service; his kingdom is not built on might but on compassion. The little donkey Jesus mounts mirrors how the prophet Zechariah foretold this scene five centuries before:

"Rejoice greatly, O daughter Zion! Shout aloud, O daughter Jerusalem! See, your king comes to you, triumphant and victorious is he, humble and riding on a donkey, on a colt, the foal of a donkey."

The Messiah-king is one with God's just — the poor and lowly of the world. Jesus' entry into Jerusalem in such a public and deeply symbolic way (which is followed immediately in Matthew's text by the routing of the money changers from the temple) sets up the final confrontation between Jesus and the chief priests and scribes.

Let the little colt of this morning's Gospel guide us through the Holy Week ahead. Let him be for us the symbol of Christ's humility — humility that is not self-loathing and self-diminishing but humility that honors all men and women as children of God, that loves all humankind as brothers and sisters in Christ, that rejoices in gratitude to God for the gift of our lives and world. In our remembering the events of Holy Week — from the upper room to Gethsemani, from Pilate's bench to Golgotha, from the cross to the empty tomb — Jesus will turn our world and its value system upside down: true authority is found in dedicated service and generosity to others; the just and loving will be exalted by God in God's time; in death we experience the fullness of life. Let the donkey and colt be our companions as we walk with Jesus and witness his passion and death this Holy Week, that we, too, may bear on our backs the servant Jesus and bear on our shoulders the cross of justice and love.

The Passion of Our Lord Jesus

The centurion and the men with him who were keeping watch over Jesus feared greatly when they saw the earthquake and all that was happening, and they said, "Truly, this was the Son of God!"

Matthew 26: 14 – 27: 66

Passion play

*W*hether the renowned production in the village of Oberammergau or a performance by school children in the parish, staging the story of Jesus' passion and death is a demanding undertaking: the many major and minor parts ... the costumes for the chief priests, the Pharisees, the soldiers ... the staging and lighting of

Gethsemani, the courtyard, Pilate's residence, Jerusalem, Golgotha ... the lighting, earthquake special effects ...

But a realistic passion play can be staged with only three actors. No special costumes or sets or effects are needed. Street clothes will do. The setting can be anywhere.

Just three actors.

The lead character might be called the *Servant*. It should be played by someone who possesses neither guile nor pretension, but be an "actor" of integrity and compassion. Throughout the play, the Servant will bring light to the dark moments of the story, healing to the members of the cast, hope as the tension builds. With a complete understanding of the intricacies of the plot, the Servant is the protagonist who struggles to bring justice, compassion, reconciliation and peace to every scene.

The second character required is best described as the *Pragmatist.* In the play, he (or she) will defend law and order, rationalize the status quo, justify the way things are. But at the bottom of the Pragmatist's every word and movement is fear: the Pragmatist is desperately afraid, afraid for himself and his security. He sees the Servant's impractical, unrealistic approach to the world to be dangerous, threatening the life the Pragmatist has worked so hard to establish for himself, his family, his community (if not exactly happy and comfortable, at least it's a life he can deal with and manage). The Pragmatist in the play is prepared to do anything he has to do to preserve the life that has worked for him, and will speak eloquently to rationalize and justify his actions.

A passion play requires one more character: the *Observer.* The Observer will watch carefully the conflict between the Servant and the Pragmatist. He (or she) will be torn by the hope and goodness of the Servant's life and the fear engendered by the Pragmatist. In the course of the play the Observer will be asked to choose — but the Observer, instead, will step back from the action, all but blending into the scenery. Eventually, the Observer will disappear from the play altogether.

Three characters are all that are needed. With those three actors, the passion is staged anywhere — in a home, in a workplace, in a schoolyard. And there will usually be some surprising and interesting improvisations of the big crucifixion scene.

The passion play is restaged in the injustice and fear all around us; it is played out in every confrontation between the things of God and the expectations of a profit-driven, me-first world. In some versions of the play, we are the Pragmatist, crushing others with our criticisms, insensitivity and selfishness. In other versions we are the Observers, watching silently as the innocent "Servants" are unjustly and unfairly betrayed, accused, condemned. And we have all taken up the cross of the Servant: We all bear nail marks on our spirits, if not our bodies, from our own experiences of crucifixion.

In every passion play, the Spirit of the God hovers as the detached Playwright and Stage Manager, writing and rewriting dialogue and directing us to our marks as we play our parts.

The course of the play is up to the actors. But the ending, in the hands of the Playwright, is always the same.

While the Blessing and Procession of Palms commemorates Jesus' triumphant entry into Jerusalem, the Liturgy of the Word focuses on the passion and death of the Messiah. In his Passion narrative, Matthew frames his account in the context of the First Testament prophecies concerning the Messiah. Matthew portrays a Jesus who is totally alone, abandoned by everyone, but who is finally vindicated by God (the portrait of the Messiah depicted in Isaiah and Psalm 22).

Scripture scholars believe that Matthew and Luke adapted their material from the evangelist Mark, whose Gospel is generally believed to have been the first to be written. Almost 80 percent of Matthew's Passion account is identical in vocabulary and content to Mark's. Matthew, however, adds several details not found in Mark's Gospel, including the death of Judas, Pilate's washing his hands of responsibility for Jesus' death, Pilate's wife's dream (throughout Matthew's Gospel, divine guidance is often revealed in dreams — Joseph's dream to take the child and his mother to Egypt, the magi's dream to flee Bethlehem), the posting of guards at the tomb after Jesus' burial.

Matthew is writing his Gospel for Jewish Christians who themselves have suffered greatly at the hands of the Jewish establishment. Many have been expelled from their synagogues and the temple for their insistent belief in Jesus as the Messiah. Jesus' trial before the Sanhedrin (the most controversial aspect of the Passion narratives historically) is pivotal in Matthew. Matthew alone names Caiaphas as high priest during the proceedings and describes in great detail the chief priests' manipulation of Pilate and the crowds. Matthew presents to his Jewish Christian community Jesus as a model of suffering at the hands of the Jews (it is Matthew's Passion account that includes the troubling line spoken by the crowds, "Let his blood be upon us and our children"). The tearing of the sanctuary veil symbolizes for Matthew's community a break with their Jewish past. (As is the case throughout Matthew's Gospel, Gentiles and not the people of Israel first recognize the truth about Jesus: only Pilate and his wife recognize the innocence of the condemned Jesus).

As we listen and pray over the story of the original Passion Play on this Passion Sunday, see the Spirit of the God, the Playwright and Stage Manager of every passion play, writing our roles in the depths of our hearts and directing us actors to the ultimate happy ending of Easter fulfillment.

*C*hrist our Redeemer,
may we not only remember
your passion, death and resurrection
this Holy Week,
but may we enter, heart and soul,
into your passion, death and resurrection.
May the example of your selfless compassion
direct our own Passion plays,
    from Jerusalem to the upper room,
    from agony to trial,
    from crucifixion to burial.

May we empty ourselves of our own hurts and wants
in order to become lights of your mercy
    and consolation for others;
may we take up our crosses as you took up yours
in the certain hope
that our experiences of crucifixion
    for the sake of justice and integrity
may be transformed into the vindication of Easter.

THE EASTER
TRIDUUM

Holy Thursday

"If I, your Teacher and Lord, washed your feet, then you must wash each other's feet."

John 13: 1–15

Holy supper

*T*raveling through a poor village in India, visitors toss scraps of food out of the bus window. Within seconds, a goat or cow wandering past disposes of a peel in a single gulp.

Two children watch as a touring bus stops at the village fruit stand. They wait and watch by the bus; as soon as the first scraps and peelings are tossed from the vehicle onto the dusty road, they pounce, retrieving four discarded banana peels. The girl, about eight years old, wears a ragged sari. She carries her little brother, who is clad only in an oversized shirt.

The girl gently puts her brother down by the side of the road. She brushes off the peels and hands all the peelings to her brother. She pulls out a grimy square cloth from the folds of her sari and smoothes it out carefully. Meticulously, the girl pulls the soft portion of each banana peel away from the outer skin and places it on the cloth. She feeds half of the sweet fruit to her brother. Then she eats. They smile and laugh and enjoy the bounty.[1]

This poor simple supper is as holy and sacred as the supper we have just read about in tonight's Gospel; the little girl, the big sister to her baby brother, mirrors Jesus the foot washer.

Christ invites us to his table, but the invitation comes with a price. To come to this table is to be both guest and servant. We are invited to feast on the bread of life and wine of salvation that is the Risen Christ — but to accept the invitation to the feast means to accept the role of servant to the other invitees: to be willing to wash the feet of one another, to carry the small and helpless among us, to share our own small helpings of banana peels with those who have nothing.

The centerpiece of John's Gospel account of the Last Supper is the *mandatum* — from the Latin word for "commandment," from which comes the traditional title for this evening, *Maundy* Thursday. At the Passover Seder, the night before he died, Jesus established a new Passover to celebrate God's covenant with the new Israel. The special character of this second covenant is the mandatum of the washing of the feet — to love one another as we have been loved by Christ.

(John makes no mention of the establishment of the Eucharist in his account of the Last Supper. Chapters 14, 15 and 16 recount Jesus' last instructions to his disciples, followed by his "high priestly prayer" in chapter 17. The Johannine theology of the Eucharist is detailed in the "bread of life" discourse following the multiplication of the loaves and fish at Passover, in chapter 6 of his Gospel.)

Jesus, who revealed the wonders of God in stories about mustard seeds, fishing nets and ungrateful children, on this last night of his life — as we know life — leaves his small band of disciples his most beautiful parable: *As I have washed your feet like a slave, so you must wash the feet of each other and serve one another. As I have loved you without limit or condition, so you must love one another without limit or condition. As I am about to suffer and die for you, so you must suffer and, if necessary, die for one another.* Tonight's parable is so simple, but its lesson is so central to what being a disciple of Christ is all about. When inspired by the love of Christ, the smallest act of service done for another takes on extraordinary dimensions.

In the sacrament that Christ institutes this last night of his life, Jesus invites us to become what we receive: to become the humble, giving Servant Christ that gives his life for us and to us in the bread and wine of the Eucharist.

*F*ather in heaven,
may we accept with humility and gratitude
the gifts your Son leaves us this night.
May we joyfully accept the towel and basin
to become foot washers for one another;
may our putting aside our own wants and needs
to wash the feet of others
make us worthy to become Jesus' second gift,
the gift of himself in the Eucharist.

Good Friday

Pilate said to Jesus, "What is truth?"

John 18: 1–19: 42

The truth in front of our eyes

"What is truth?" Pilate asks Jesus.

And Jesus doesn't answer.

Or Pilate doesn't give Jesus a chance to answer.

Is Pilate asking a serious question here?

Or is Pilate expressing his exasperation at the whole question of "truth"? It's understandable. Since he took his post as governor of this remote end of the vast Roman empire, Pilate has been accosted with so many systems and images of truth — from the ancient religious traditions of the Jews to the political demands of his imperial bosses. Now here is this poor, pathetic figure in front of him proclaiming yet another version of truth — this time truth about a kingdom somewhere out there beyond the world. Pilate has had a belly full of "truth."

And so have we. We are assailed with so many perspectives and opinions all claiming to be the "truth" — the truth about medical ethics, about sexual morality, about economic and environmental justice.

It's getting hard to see exactly what is the "truth" — even when it's standing right in front of you.

Today, truth is standing in front of us in the figure of the humiliated Jesus, the suffering Jesus, the ridiculed Jesus, the crucified Jesus. Right in front of us is the truth about a God who loves us to a degree we cannot begin to fathom; a God who refuses to give up or reject or destroy his beloved creation — a creation that has hardly lived up to its promise; a God who humbles himself to become one of us in order to make us like him, to realize that we have been created in his image, created by his very breath blown into our hearts.

"What is truth?"

The answer to Pilate's question is not simple; it is not black and white.

Truth is profound and complex; it is of every shade of gray and of every color of the spectrum.

Truth is not easy; it is not comforting.

Truth is demanding and challenging.

But truth begins here, at the cross of God's own Son.

Truth is rooted in the tree on which hangs Jesus, the very compassion of God.

In the light of Good Friday, truth begins to become a little clearer …

*F*ather of compassion,
enlighten our conflicted minds
    and open our closed spirits
to embrace the truth that stands before us
    on this Good Friday:
that you have called us to be a people
of your love and compassion,
that you have formed us to be a church
of reconciliation and forgiveness,
that you have sent us to realize your dream
of a human family united in justice and peace.
Give us the wisdom and patience,
the perseverance and conviction,
to embrace the truth revealed in the cross
and to allow that truth
to transform all of our Good Fridays
into Easter mornings.

The angel said to the woman, "Do not be afraid! I know that you are seeking Jesus the crucified. He is not here, for he has been raised up just as he said … "

Matthew 28: 1–10

Grasped by the hand of Christ

*F*or centuries, the Eastern churches have celebrated and preserved their faith in *icons* — paintings of Christ, the Virgin Mary, the saints and scenes from the Gospel that are stunning in their simple beauty and simplicity. What differentiates true icons from other religious paintings is that icons are not painted but "copied" — artists "copy" or "write" icons whose origins date back to antiquity.

One of the oldest and most revered icons of the Eastern Church is a motif of Jesus' descent into hell. Since antiquity, iconographers have "copied" the scene of Jesus standing on the battered-down doors of hell and extending his hands to a man and woman, representing Adam and Eve, to take them from the darkness of hell into the light of heaven. Locks and chains, symbols of bondage, float mysteriously in a vast black space below the figures.

If you look closely at the icon, you see that Christ's taking of Adam and Eve's hands is not merely an affectionate clasp of hands — Christ *grabs* Adam and Eve by the wrists and forcefully *pulls* them out of their tombs into the freedom of his resurrection. In some renditions of this icon, Adam's expression suggests not only surprise but confusion — it's almost as if he is not sure he wants to be freed from his place in hell.

It is a telling detail. God will not be dissuaded from being reconciled with his beloved creation. In Christ, God takes the initiative in our salvation; he makes the first and last move in our

---

redemption. Compelled by the unfathomable love that is uniquely of God, God humbles himself to become human like us, putting aside his divinity to begin his "pulling" us into eternity.

Whether we want to be so loved or not.

The icon portrays ultimate hope: God loves us, despite ourselves; God's love triumphs over all, even death; God's love re-creates, transforms, makes new.

The lesson of the icon is that Resurrection is not always a gentle or immediately welcomed experience. There is a certain sense of security and safety in our confinement: Within our "tombs" we know the boundaries, we know the limits, we have learned how to exist and make life work within our enclosed space. But now along comes the Easter Christ to tear down the safe, protective walls we have erected, to pull us out of our tombs and into the full light of life.

Like the icon, Matthew's Gospel presents Jesus' resurrection as a great intervention by God, inaugurating a new order throughout creation and history. The empty tomb is surrounded by miraculous phenomena: the earthquake, the angel whose appearance resembles a "flash of lightning" with garments as "dazzling as snow," the rolled back stone and the collapse of the guards.

In Matthew's account, Mary Magdalene and the "other" Mary come to the tomb for no other reason than to mourn (the guards, no doubt, would have prevented any attempt to go near the body for additional anointing). The disciples, meanwhile, are nowhere to be seen. The women's courageous and compassionate presence is rewarded by their being the first to hear the astonishing news of the Resurrection. The angel explains that Jesus has been "raised up" exactly as he prophesied on three occasions in Matthew's Gospel (16: 21, 17:23 and 20:19). The two women then become "apostles to the apostles," sent to tell the others what they have seen.

In the Easter miracle, God re-creates the world. It is the first night and day of the second Genesis. Death is no longer the ultimate finality but the ultimate beginning. The Christ who taught forgiveness, who pleaded for reconciliation, who handed himself over to his executioners for the sake of justice and mercy, has been raised up by God. We leave behind in the grave our sinfulness, our dark side, our selfishness, our pettiness — the evil that mars God's first creation.

In the light of Easter morning, we realize unmistakably the depth of God's love for us and understand the profound truth of Jesus' Gospel of compassion, love, forgiveness, reconciliation and selflessness for the sake of others. God's "raising up" of his Son affirms our redemption through the power of the Gospel spirit of love; the empty tomb of Easter is the ultimate victory of the Gospel over humanity's sad tendency toward despair, isolation, prejudice and selfishness.

*F*ather, tonight we celebrate the empty tomb
    of your Son —
your ultimate promise of hope, of life, of love
    to humanity.
May the joy of this night give us the grace and hope
to abandon the tombs we create for ourselves
and bring the resurrection into this life of ours;
to renew and re-create our world in the light
    of the Risen Christ;
to proclaim in every moment of our lives
the Gospel of the Holy One, Christ Jesus,
who has died, who has risen, and who comes again!

EASTER

Easter Sunday

On the first day of the week, Mary of Magdala came to the tomb early in the morning, when it was still dark ...

John 20: 1–9

First light

John's Easter story begins in the early morning darkness.

This is always how our discovery of the Risen Christ begins — in *darkness.*

While it is still dark, Mary Magdalene goes to the tomb of the Jesus who healed her, who taught her, who accorded her respect and love she never thought herself worthy of. With his death, her hope died.

In the week past, someone's hope was crucified. And the darkness is overwhelming:

Someone was called into her supervisor's office and was told that, because of the brutal economy, she is being let go. She cleaned out her desk and packed away her hope. She walked into the darkness of wondering what she will tell her kids.

Someone received a death sentence from his physician.

Someone else heard the words from her spouse, *I don't love you anymore.*

Someone sat alone waiting for a son or daughter to come home.

No one is ready to encounter Easter until he or she has spent time in the early morning darkness where hope cannot be seen. In such darkness, Easter is the last thing we are expecting. And that is why Easter terrifies us. We dread the darkness, but we fear even more what is beyond it. Sometimes the darkness we know is preferable to what we don't know — we have learned at least to function and exist in the darkness; we find a distorted solace in the fact that darkness means nothing more can disappoint or hurt us.

In our darkness, we are not ready for Easter's first light. It illuminates those dark places we have become used to, it reveals what we have never seen before, it dares us imagine possibilities beyond our limited understanding of what is possible.[1]

And so John begins his Easter story in the darkness. The evangelist John is the master dramatist. As seen this Lent in John's stories of the Samaritan woman at the well, the healing of the man born blind, and the raising of Lazarus from the dead, John centers his narrative on the reaction of people to Jesus' words or actions. John's Easter Gospel is a case in point. John's account contains nothing of earthquakes or angels. In the darkness before daybreak, Mary of Magdala, following the Jewish custom of visiting the tomb during this three-day period, goes to the tomb to discover that the stone has been moved away and the burial cloths are neatly folded. She runs to tell Peter and the others. Peter and the "other disciple" race to get there and look inside. John's narrative focuses on the different reactions of the three: Mary fears that someone has "taken" Jesus' body; Peter does not know what to make of the news; but the "other" disciple — the model of faithful discernment in John's Gospel — immediately understands what has taken place. So great are the disciple's love and depth of faith that all of the strange remarks and dark references of Jesus now become clear to him.

Today we stand, with Peter and John and Mary, at the entrance of the empty tomb; with them, we wonder what it means. God has raised up his Christ. All that he taught — compassion, love, forgiveness, reconciliation, sincerity, selflessness for the sake of others — is vindicated and affirmed if he is truly risen. The empty tomb calls us out of the darkness that shrouds our lives and into the light of possibility, of healing, of re-creation. In his rising from the dead, Christ enables us to bring into our own lives all that he taught and lived throughout his life — the love, compassion, generosity, humility and selflessness that ultimately triumphs over hatred, bigotry, prejudice, despair, greed — and even death.

The empty tomb is the sign of perfect hope — that in Christ all things are possible, that we can make of our lives what we want them to be, that we can become the people God created us to be.

Easter morning's first light calls us to rise from our fear of Resurrection and the promise of the Risen One who is forever in our midst.

*F*ather, we celebrate the empty tomb of your Son —
your ultimate promise to us of hope, of life, of love.
May the joy of this Easter morning give us the grace
to abandon the tombs we create for ourselves
and bring the resurrection into this life of ours;
to walk out of the darkness of our fears and hurts
and renew and re-create our world
    in the light of the Risen Christ;
to proclaim in every moment of our lives
    the Gospel of the Holy One,
Christ Jesus who has died, who has risen, and who
    comes again!

[NOTE: The Gospel from the Easter Vigil
may be read on Easter Sunday.]

Second Sunday of Easter

"Peace be with you. As the Father has sent me, so I send you. And when he said this he breathed upon them and said to them, "Receive the Holy Spirit …"
Jesus said to Thomas, "Put your finger here and see my hands, and bring your hand and put it into my side, and do not be unbelieving, but believe."

John 20: 19–31

Nail marks

*I*t has happened to all of us. We discover that we are better people than we think we are.

The parish puts out a call for volunteers. There aren't enough hours in the day as it is — and you can't imagine yourself contributing anything meaningful to help the elderly, the homeless, the poor, or kids — especially (God help us!) teenagers. But once you begin, you find a real joy working with these folks. You look forward to these couple of hours. You realize that you have been changed as much as those you have touched.

Or you walk into the cafeteria and the only place left is a seat next to her. She's nice enough but painfully shy — she barely says hello to anyone. You sit down and say *Hi*. You're taken back by the welcome and graciousness in her quiet *Hello*. The ice is broken; a friendship begins — all because you were willing to risk a simple *Hello*.

Or a beloved family member or friend is critically ill. You feel helpless. You'd like to go and be with them — but you're afraid you may say the wrong thing and upset them beyond consolation; you fear that in your clumsiness and awkwardness you may do more harm than good. But it becomes clear in just a few seconds that your presence alone has brought much joy to the dying, that your simple taking of their hand reassures them that they are loved and cared for.

In today's Gospel, the Risen Christ invites the doubting Thomas to place his fingers "in the nail marks" and "in my side" and believe — believe in the love of God to transform us and in the grace to be agents of that love for others. The "nail marks" of Jesus are all around us in the lives of those walking their own Calvarys.

The story of Thomas' encounter with the Risen Jesus is the second of two stories that make up today's pericope from John's Gospel.

The first story takes place on Easter night. The terrified disciples are huddled together behind locked doors. They are marked men because of their association with the criminal Jesus. The Risen Jesus appears in their midst with his greeting of "peace." John clearly has the Genesis story in mind when the evangelist describes Jesus as "breathing" the Holy Spirit on his disciples: Just as God created man and woman by breathing life into them (Genesis 2: 7), the Risen Christ re-creates humankind by breathing the new life of the Holy Spirit upon the eleven.

The "peace" that Christ gives his new Church is not a sedative of good feeling or the simple absence of conflict or hostility. Christ's peace is active and transforming; it re-creates and renews. It is peace that is born of gratitude and humility, peace that values the hopes and dreams and needs of another over one's own, peace that welcomes back the lost, heals the brokenhearted, and respects the dignity of every man, woman and child as a son and daughter of God. Christ's peace is hard work; creating and maintaining the peace of Christ requires focused and determined action.

We trace our roots as a parish to that Easter night. Jesus' "breathing" his spirit of peace and reconciliation upon his frightened disciples transformed them into a new creation, the Church. Jesus' gift of peace and his entrusting to his disciples the work of forgiveness defines the very identity of a church, a parish, a community of faith: to accept one another, to affirm one another, to support one another as God has done for us in the Risen Christ.

What brought the Eleven and the first Christians together as a community — unity of heart, missionary witness, prayer, works of charity, a commitment to reconciliation and forgiveness — no less powerfully binds us to one another as the Church of the Risen Christ today.

Which leads into the story of Thomas. The disciples excitedly tell the just-returned Thomas of what they had seen. Thomas responds to the news with understandable skepticism. A week later, Jesus returns to the gathering of disciples — this time with Thomas present. He invites Thomas to examine his wounds and to "believe." Christ's blessing in response to Thomas' profession of faith exalts the faith of every Christian of every age who "believes without seeing," who realizes and celebrates the presence of the Risen Christ in their midst by living lives of Gospel compassion, justice and forgiveness. In raising his beloved Son from the dead, God also raises our spirits to the realization of the totality and limitlessness of his love for us.

While "doubting Thomas" will take his lumps from many pulpits this Sunday, his reaction is understandable. It is natural to approach any degree of change with skepticism and doubt. Whatever is new we greet initially with a healthy dose of skepticism; whatever challenges our usual way of doing things is rejected out of hand and scorned; whatever threatens our safe, comfortable approach to life must be neutralized before it can turn our world upside down. We have all been disappointed, bamboozled and ridiculed too many times. There's more than a little "doubting Thomas" in all of us.

The signs of resurrection are all around us: the "nail marks" of sufferings endured that have led to the victory of justice and righteousness; empty tombs from which souls dead to fear and hopelessness have risen to new possibilities. Our own passion experiences call us to move beyond the betrayals and injustices that we have endured. With an openness of heart and generosity of spirit, with perseverant faith in God's ever-present grace, wonderful things are possible, dreams worthy of our hope can be realized, resurrection can take place in our own time and place. As Thomas experiences, Easter transforms our crippling sense of skepticism and cynicism into a sense of trust and hope in the providence of God. The power of the Resurrection transcends time and place.

*B*reathe your Spirit of peace
into our tired, withered souls, O Risen One:
that we may be re-created in Easter hope;
that we may be healed of our hurts and disappointments
in our struggle to be your disciples;
that we may be transformed into your church of peace,
ministers of your forgiveness
and witnesses of your resurrection
to our broken, crucified world.

Third Sunday of Easter

Two of Jesus disciples were going to a village seven miles from Jerusalem called Emmaus, and they were conversing about all the things that had occurred. And it happened that Jesus himself drew near and walked with them, but their eyes were prevented from recognizing him.

Luke 24: 13–35

The many roads to Emmaus

A mother and father rush their child to the hospital in the middle of the night. They have done everything they could think of, but the baby's fever will not go down. It is a long night of waiting, of second-guessing, of desperate prayers. From their child's room to the hospital, from the emergency room to the waiting room, this young mother and father walk the long road to Emmaus.

While not a complete surprise, it was still a blow. Her job was one of many that were eliminated in a company's "reduction in work force." There would be a modest severance package, of course, and some outplacement help, but to find another job in her field at her salary would mean a move to another city — or she would have to "retool" and begin a new career. So begins her own journey to Emmaus.

He had taken a year off from school to work on the campaign. He believed in what the candidate stood for, in the political process, in the ideal that one person could make a difference. But after a bruising campaign, his candidate lost the election. The young campaign worker's idealism also took a beating as he saw for the first time how ugly politics can be. *What's next?* he wonders, as he begins the next chapter of his life and career along the road to Emmaus.

We have all traveled the road the two disciples walked that Easter night: the road of deep disappointment, sadness, despair, anger — but it is also a road in which we meet the Risen One in the guise of those who offer us support, compassion and counsel along the way.

Today's Gospel begins on the afternoon of that miraculous Easter Sunday. Having just completed the observance of the Passover Sabbath, two disciples of Jesus (one identified as Cleopas) are making the seven-mile trip to the village of Emmaus. By identifying them as disciples, Luke is emphasizing that these two were more than just disinterested observers of the events of Holy Week. Their conversation must have been punctuated by shock, anger and sadness over the great injustice that had befallen their revered Rabbi Jesus.

The two are suddenly joined by a stranger who asks what they are talking about with such passion. The stranger then explains, to their astonishment, the meaning of each of the events of the past week. When they reach the village, the two disciples ask the stranger to stay with them. And, in the words from Luke's Gospel that we have come to treasure, the two disciples "come to know (the Risen Christ) in the breaking of the bread."

It is said that true friendship begins when friends share a memory. Like the two disciples who recognize Jesus in the breaking of bread, we, too, are bound as a church by the same memory of the Risen One. In the word we hear and the bread we share, God's love is both remembered and relived, giving us hope and direction and meaning in the course of our individual journeys.

At the Last Supper table in the Cenacle, at the table in the inn at Emmaus, at the table in our own parish church, disciples of every time and place encounter the Risen Christ in the "breaking of the bread." But the Eucharist is as much a verb as a noun — it is something that we *do*. In this sacrament, we become what we consume: We become the compassion and humility, the justice and peace, of the Gospel. The Eucharist that begins on Sunday extends into the rest of the week; the Christ we meet here walks with us on our Monday-through-Saturday journeys to our own Emmauses. In coming "to know him in the breaking of bread," our lives experience the peace and hope possible only in his Resurrection.

*J*ourney with us, Lord Jesus;
Be our companion and guest
as we walk our everyday roads to Emmaus.
May your light guide us on our way
and your Gospel be the markings we follow.
May the bread we break in memory of you
sustain us on our journey to the dwelling place
    of your Father.

"I am the gate. Whoever enters through me will be saved and will come in and go out and find pasture."

John 10: 1–10

That's my dad, the guardrail

If you've ever cared for a baby who has just discovered mobility, you quickly realize that sometimes you have to use anything and everything to keep the little crawling dynamo from open doors and flights of stairs. While gates and playpens are effective deterrents to a point, the most effective guardrail is often *you*. Many a child's first steps are made within the safety of a parent's own curled body and extended arms and legs.

The Gospel for the Third Sunday of Easter each year is taken from Chapter 10 of John's Gospel, Jesus' "Good Shepherd" discourse. In today's pericope, two kinds of sheepfolds or corrals are mentioned. The first is a community sheepfold in each town and locale, a large enclosure that would house several flocks of sheep. The town's gatekeeper knew each flock's owner and shepherd; each flock knew the voice of their own shepherd and would know to follow him to the grazing pastures.

The second sheepfold is the shepherd himself. During Jesus' time, shepherds protected their flocks, literally, with their own bodies. Sheepfolds were formed by loosely piled stones. In the wall was a single, narrow opening. The "gate" was the shepherd himself. At night, he would sleep in the middle of that opening. Any sheep wanting to wander out or any thief trying to get in would have to go through the shepherd first.

Both "gates" mirror the Redeemer Christ, the "Good Shepherd" who lays down his own life in order to become the very source of life for his people: When our spirits ache over what has been lost, when we lose our moral and ethical way, when we feel our footing slip beneath us as we try to navigate life's twists and turns, Christ's voice can always be heard above the noise and din of our lives if we listen for it with hope, conviction and faith; he is the gate, passage way, that leads us to the life of God, to discerning the way of God in all things.

There is another important dimension to this discourse. John places these words of Jesus right after the curing of the man born blind (the Gospel read a few weeks ago on the Fourth Sunday of Lent). The evangelist uses Jesus' images of shepherds, sheep and sheep gates to underline the miserable job of "shepherding" being done by the Pharisees and the temple authorities as in the case of the blind man. John echoes the warning of the prophet Ezekiel (Ezekiel 34): God will raise up a new shepherd to replace the irresponsible and "thieving" shepherds who feed themselves at the expense of the flock. Today's Gospel, then, is a lesson in servanthood: Jesus calls us to listen for and follow his "voice" to imitate his "shepherding" of selfless compassion.

*J*esus the Good Shepherd,
guide our steps over the crags and rocky terrain
     of our lives,
and bring us safely to the pasture
of your wisdom and grace.
Make us selfless shepherds to one another,
that we may walk with them through the gate
of your peace and compassion.

Fifth Sunday of Easter

"I am the way and the truth and the life. No one comes to the Father except through me ... Whoever believes in me will do the works that I do, and will do greater than these, because I am going to the Father."

John 14: 1–12

Sacred knitting

A group of women meet one or two evenings a week. They light a candle and offer a prayer together, perhaps sing a hymn. Then they begin their sacred work:

Knitting.

The women are part of a ministry that has touched many lives in churches and parishes across the country. They knit and crochet prayer shawls. The shawls are then given to parishioners coping with crisis, illness or need. The birth of a child, an illness, the death of a loved one — all are occasions for the "hug" in the shape of a shawl. While stitching, the maker of the shawl holds that person who will be receiving it in her thoughts, making the very act of knitting a prayer.

Those who receive the shawls say that they feel loved, cared for and, most of all, surrounded by God's love and compassion. They are deeply moved to know that someone has cared enough to pray for them and to make a cozy, warm, comforting gift. The mother of a young girl battling cancer told the knitters in her parish that her daughter said that when she felt bad, she wrapped herself up tightly in the shawl and it made her feel better. Another woman refused to take her shawl off during her final months of life because it was her "scarf of love." Many who have known the solace of a prayer shawl in their last months ask to be buried with the shawl around their shoulders.

But the knitters believe that they receive as much from making the shawls as do those who receive them. Their simple knitting and gentle prayer become offerings and symbols of God's compassion for others — and God is as present to them as they knit as he is to those who will wrap themselves up in the loving warmth of the shawl itself.[2]

The simplest work of compassion and charity, done in God's spirit of love, is to do the very work of Christ; the most hidden and unseen acts of kindness will be exalted by Christ as great in the kingdom of his Father. On the night before he died (the setting of today's Gospel), Jesus asks his disciples to take up "the work that I do" — the work of humble servanthood that places the hurts and pain of others before our own, the work of charity that does not measure the cost, the work of love that transcends limits and conditions. In his example of humble, selfless love, Jesus is "the way and the truth and the life"; in embracing his spirit of humble servanthood, we make our way to the Father.

John's account of that final night of Jesus' life is the longest in the Gospels — five chapters in length (but with no account of the institution of the Eucharist). The evangelist uses a literary device common in Scripture: A leader (Moses, Joshua, David, Tobit) gathers his own (family, friends, disciples) to announce his imminent departure, offer advice and insight into the future and give final instructions. The dominant themes here are consolation and encouragement: *Be faithful to God's Word and Law; remember and live what I have taught you, for better days are ahead for you.*

From John's Gospel, it is clear that the disciples do not comprehend the full import of what Jesus is telling them. While still envisioning the establishment of a political, Jesus-led kingdom supplanting their hated Roman occupiers, a frustrated Jesus reiterates in the clearest language and imagery of John's Gospel that his "kingdom" is one of spirit, a domain that transcends the physical and embraces human hearts.

God is in our midst; God is present in every "work" of reconciliation, justice and peace; God lives in the most hidden and unheralded acts of charity and selflessness. Even the knitting of a shawl, when taken up in the humble compassion of the Gospel Jesus, becomes a sacred act, a participation in the "work that I do."

*G*uide our hands, O Lord,
that every project and work we undertake
may be part of your work of generosity.

Illuminate our minds, O Lord,
that every word we utter
may be part of your work of peace and justice.

Open our hearts, O Lord,
That every comfort we offer,
every quiet moment of consolation we extend,
may be part of your work of compassion.

In simplicity and humility,
may everything we do be part of the sacred work
the Father entrusted to you
and you now entrust to us.

Sixth Sunday of Easter

" ... the Father will give you another Advocate to be with you always, the Spirit of truth, whom the world cannot accept, because it neither sees nor knows him."

John 14: 15–21

Reunion

The four of them met on their first day at college when they found themselves sitting at the same cafeteria table at breakfast. Thrown into the excitement and terror of the college experience, they helped each other make it through those first few days. Together they forged their way through the next four years: unfathomable lectures, mysterious lab experiments, autocratic professors, midnight study sessions. They pulled one another through the trauma of broken romances and the mornings after the nights before. They toasted grad school acceptances, first jobs and engagements.

Commencement only deepened their friendship. They were always there for one another, through good times and bad. They celebrated one another's marriages, welcomed their children, mourned break-ups and helped one another cope with their first real experiences of death and loss. The four knew that help, support and understanding were only a phone call way — always honest and blunt, never judgmental or condemning.

This year the four will meet at their *alma mater* for their 25th reunion. They are older, grayer and wiser than that first breakfast. But the experiences they shared and the memories they cherish make their friendship as strong and as real as the morning it first took root a quarter of a century ago. When they meet on the Friday night of reunion weekend, they will pick up the conversation as if they had never been separated.

Shared memories are what bind friends together. A shared memory is what binds us together as a Church: the memory we share and celebrate in the event of Christ — a memory that is as real and as strong among us today as it was for the Twelve that Holy Thursday night in the Cenacle. The Spirit of Truth, the Paraclete, is the creative, living memory of the Church. The Spirit/Paraclete unites us and energizes us as we come together to share, re-live and learn from our memory of the Risen Christ. Jesus — the wise Rabbi, the compassionate Healer, the Friend of the rich and poor and the saint and sinner, the obedient and humble Servant of God — is a living presence among us who makes of us a community of faith, a family, a circle of friends who offer Christ's love, support and compassion to one another.

In legal terminology, an advocate defends the accused at trial. For John, Christ is the first "Advocate," who comes to liberate humanity from the imprisonment and condemnation of sin. The second "Advocate," promised by Jesus in today's Gospel, is the "Spirit of truth," the Church's living, creative memory in which the mystery of God's love, revealed by and in Christ, lives for all time. This Spirit of truth, "whom the world cannot accept," illuminates our vision and opens our hearts to discern the will and wisdom of God. The Spirit "advocates" within us for what is good, right and just, despite the skepticism and rejection of those who are blind to what is good.

Throughout his Gospel, John never allows love, as taught by Jesus, to remain at the level of sentiment or emotion. Love compels us to embrace the attitude of Christ, the humble servant of God; love opens our spirits to behold the image of God in one another. To love as Jesus loved — in total and selfless obedience, without conditions and without expectation of that love ever being returned — is the difficult love that Jesus expects of those who claim to be his disciples.

Make us one, Lord Jesus,
in the memory of your great love for us.
May the memory of your humility in becoming one of us,
the memory of your compassion to poor and hurting,
the memory of your confronting the unjust
    and self-centered,
the memory of your teachings that inspired
    joy and hope,
the memory of your sacrifice of yourself for our sake,
be a living reality for us, your Church.
May that memory of you
be celebrated at our parish altar
where you touch our souls in the Eucharist,
and at our family tables where we welcome you
in welcoming and loving one another.

Ascension of the Lord

"You will receive power when the Holy Spirit comes upon you, and you will be my witnesses ... to the ends of the earth."

Acts 1: 1–11

"Go and make disciples of all nations, baptizing them ... and teaching them to observe all that I have commanded you."

Matthew 28: 16–20

Toasting Mem and Pop

*O*n the evening of their 50ᵗʰ wedding anniversary, their children hosted a dinner party for their parents at a downtown restaurant. They invited some two hundred relatives and friends.

From the guest list, it was clear how many lives the couple had touched. There were their beloved children and grandchildren who adored "Mem" and "Pop," as well as brothers and sisters and cousins. Many friends from their church came, including those she had taught in religious education over the years and those for whom she knitted shawls as part of the church's Prayer Shawl Ministry; and families he had helped in his work with the St. Vincent de Paul Society and his brother Knights of Columbus. The party included former students from her 35 years of teaching high school math and clients and employees from his printing business. At a special table were seated those precious and dearest friends they had known from their childhoods. And then there were the friends of their children who considered them second parents.

People of every background, culture, social class, ideology and belief-system came to celebrate this wonderful couple and had come to toast them on their anniversary. People who would never meet or associate or come together were brought together this night, bound together by their love and affection for this couple, grateful for the blessings of compassion, understanding and support "Mem" and "Pop" had brought to their lives.

As they raise their glasses to toast the couple, they are a community, a family.

Like the guests gathering together to celebrate this beloved couple, our own Church "works" because of the constant presence of Jesus. He brings us together as Church; his presence binds us together into this community of faith. In him, we find unity in the midst of diversity; reason to love and forgive in the busyness of our very different lives. It is not an abstract or distant presence — Christ is the center of our Church in word, in sacrament, in every moment of generosity and every act of compassion we perform and experience. In imitating his selflessness, in embracing his Gospel of reconciliation and justice, we are bound together into the body of the Risen One— even with folks we don't like or disagree with or would rather have nothing to do with.

The Ascension of the Lord is not the marking of a departure but the celebration of a presence:

Today's first reading is the beginning of the Acts of the Apostles, Luke's "Gospel of the Holy Spirit." Jesus' ascension begins volume two of Luke's work. The words and images here are similar to the First Testament accounts of the ascension of Elijah (2 Kings 2) and the forty years of the Exodus: Luke (invoking the sacred number of forty) considers the time that the Risen Lord spent with his disciples a sacred time, a "desert experience" for the apostles to prepare them for their new ministry of preaching the Gospel of the resurrection. (Acts alone places the Ascension forty days after Easter; the synoptic Gospels — including, strangely, Luke's own Gospel — specifically place the Ascension on the day of Easter; John writes of the "ascension" not as an event but as a new existence with the Father.)

Responding to their question about the restoration of Israel, Jesus discourages his disciples from guessing what cannot be known. Greater things await them as his "witnesses." In the missionary work before them, Christ will be with them in the presence of the promised Spirit.

Matthew's Gospel begins with the promise of Emmanuel — *God is with us;* it concludes with the promise of the Risen Christ, *I am with you always, even to the end of time.* Jesus' Ascension is both an ending and a beginning. The physical appearances of Jesus are at an end; his revelation of the "good news" is complete; the promise of the Messiah is fulfilled. Now begins the work of the disciples to teach what they have learned and to share what they have witnessed. While Jesus returns to the Father from whom he comes, he remains present to us in the Spirit of his love, his hope, his compassion.

*M*ay we always realize your presence in our midst,
O Risen Lord,
as we struggle to go forth
and do the work you have left us:
to teach others, in the example of our lives,
your Gospel of forgiveness and compassion,
to restore to our world
the peace and justice of your Father's kingdom,
to bring all nations and peoples together
under your commandment of love.

[In some churches and dioceses, the Ascension of the Lord
is celebrated on the Seventh Sunday of Easter.]

"Now this is eternal life, that they should know you, the only true God, and the one whom you sent, Jesus Christ. " ... the words you gave to me I have given to them, and they accepted them and truly understood that I came from you, and they have believed that you sent me. I pray for them."

John 17: 1–11

Last prayers

*L*ate morning is Amelia's favorite time of the day. The Hospice volunteers have helped Amelia get washed and dressed. After preparing her breakfast, they go quietly about whatever household tasks need to be done. That gives Amelia this quiet time in her sun room.

Amelia is at peace. She is grateful for the days she has left. In this quiet time every morning, she fingers her rosary, but the photographs of her family that cover the table near her rocker are her real prayer beads. She picks each one up gently. She prays that her son will do well in his new job ... that her daughter continues to conquer the challenges of her medical training ... that her grandson will choose the right college and grow into adulthood ... that her granddaughter will be born whole and healthy.

"Hold them all, O Lord, in your hand," Amelia prays. "Bless them as you have blessed my husband and me these many years."

Today Jesus prays for the Church he leaves behind. The same anxieties and hopes that Amelia voices in her prayers for those she loves and is about to leave behind Jesus voices in his prayers for those he loves and will leave behind. In this touching scene from John's Last Supper account, we see and hear Jesus commending every disciple of every time and place — and that includes you and me — to his Father.

The Church as a community of prayer is at the heart of today's readings — prayer that is, first and foremost, an attitude of trust and acceptance of God's presence in the community, an attitude that is not occasional but constant and continuing, an attitude not limited to asking for what is not or remains undone but also of thanksgiving for what is and for what has been. The prayer of Jesus at the Last Supper and the prayer of the company of disciples seek not God's acquiescence to their will but that God's will might be accomplished through them.

In the first part of what has become known as Jesus' "high priestly prayer" (today's pericope from John 17), Jesus prays that his disciples will be worthy and effective witnesses of the Gospel he has entrusted to them. When Jesus left this world, he had little reason to hope. He seemed to have achieved so little and to have won so few. And the Twelve — soon to be the Eleven — to whom he has entrusted his new Church, are certainly not among the most gifted of leaders nor the most dynamic of preachers. Yet with so small a beginning, Jesus changed the world. As Jesus returns to the Father, he leaves a portion of the Father's glory behind: the community of faith.

Jesus prays not only for his followers at table with him then but also for us at this table: that we may be united and consecrated in the truth Jesus has revealed and that we may reveal to the world the love and care of the Father for all of the human family. In his "high priestly prayer," we behold our connectedness to the Church of all times and places: from the Risen Christ's greeting of peace Easter night to our own *Alleluias* this Easter. As Amelia gathers her family in prayer, may we gather one another, always and everywhere, into prayer before the God to whom we all belong, who gives us all things in Christ.

$\mathcal{M}$ay we give your glory, O Lord,
by taking on the work you gave us to do:

to reveal your living presence
in the midst of our families and communities,
to speak your word of compassion and forgiveness
 to all,
to bring all men and women back to you,
you who are Father of all and Author of everything
 that is good.

Pentecost

All of them were filled with the Holy Spirit and began to speak in other languages, as the Spirit gave them ability.

Acts 2: 1–11

Jesus breathed on them and said: "Receive the Holy Spirit … "

John 20: 19–23

Realizations

*R*emember the moment when you understood — fully comprehended — that 2 + 2 = 4? Or the first time you were able to put letters together to make words and sound them out to actually read? A whole new world opened up before you.

Or the day you got your driver's license and the first time you took to the road by yourself — without Dad or Mom or the driving instructor in the passenger seat watching every maneuver you made? It was your first real sense of independence and power.

How about the first big project you headed up for your company, the first big case you won, the first big sale you made, the first class you taught? You never worked harder on anything in your life. It was as if everything you had studied had been designed to prepare you for this singular success. What you had seen and heard in the classroom and laboratory had now become real.

Will you ever forget the moment you realized you were in love with the person who became your spouse? All of the things that attracted you to this person — from that beautiful smile to such God-like compassion — led you to understand that this is the person you wanted to spend the rest of your life with. You experienced love in all its beauty — and terror.

In the Pentecost event, the faith that they had received and the wonders they had witnessed came together for the Twelve (Matthias has already been chosen to take Judas' place in the company). Pentecost was a moment of clarity and understanding; it was a moment of resolve to begin the work that Jesus entrusted to them to establish God's kingdom on earth.

Pentecost was the Jewish festival of the harvest (also called the Feast of Weeks), celebrated 50 days after Passover, when the first fruits of the corn harvest were offered to the Lord. A feast of pilgrimage (hence the presence in Jerusalem of so many "devout Jews of every nation"), Pentecost also commemorated Moses' receiving the Law on Mount Sinai. For the new Israel, Pentecost becomes the celebration of the Spirit of God's compassion, peace and forgiveness — the Spirit that transcends the Law and becomes the point of departure for the young Church's universal mission.

In his Acts of the Apostles (Reading 1), Luke evokes the Old Testament images of wind and fire in his account of the new Church's Pentecost: God frequently revealed his presence in fire (the pillar of fire in the Sinai) and in wind (the wind that sweeps over the earth to make the waters of the Great Flood subside). The Hebrew word for spirit *ruah* and the Greek word *pneuma* also refer to the movement of air, not only as wind, but also of life-giving breath (as in God's creation of man in Genesis 2 and the revivification of the dry bones in Ezekiel 37). Through his life-giving "breath," the Lord begins the era of the new Israel on Pentecost.

Today's Gospel is the first appearance of the Risen Jesus before his ten disciples (remember Thomas is not present) on Easter night is John's version of the Pentecost event. In "breathing" the Holy Spirit upon them, Jesus imitates God's act of creation in Genesis. Just as Adam's life came from God, so the disciples' new life of the Spirit comes from Jesus. In the Resurrection, the Spirit replaces their sense of self-centered fear and confusion with the "peace" of understanding, enthusiasm and joy and shatters all barriers among them to make of them a community of hope and forgiveness. By Christ's sending them forth, the disciples become *apostles* — "those sent."

In Jesus' breathing upon the assembled disciples on Easter night the new life of the Spirit, the community of the Resurrection — the Church — takes flight. That same Spirit continues to "blow" through our experience of Church to give life and direction to our mission and ministry to preach the Gospel to every nation, to proclaim forgiveness and reconciliation in God's name, to immerse all of humanity into the life and love of God manifested in Jesus' Resurrection.

The feast of Pentecost celebrates the unseen, immeasurable presence of God in our lives and in our Church — the *ruah* that animates us to do the work of Gospel justice and mercy, the *ruah* that makes God's will our will, the *ruah* of God living in us and transforming us so that we might bring his life and love to our broken world. God "breathes" his Spirit into our souls that we may live in his life and love; God ignites the "fire" of his Spirit within our hearts and minds that we may seek God in all things in order to realize the coming of his reign.

*C*ome, Spirit of God
and breathe your *ruah* through your Church.
Animate us to love as you have loved us.
Inspire us to follow your example
    of humble and gracious servanthood.
Compel us to seek your justice and mercy in all things.
Come, Holy Spirit,
re-create us in the peace of the Risen One,
that we may become the realization of Christ's vision
of a Church of compassion and forgiveness.

Solemnities Of the Lord in Ordinary Time

The Holy Trinity

"God so loved the world that he gave his only Son ... for God did not send his Son into the world to condemn the world but that the world might be saved through him."

John 3: 16–18

Root, branch and fruit

A seed is a miraculous thing: so small you can barely see it, and yet containing within it the power to become the mightiest oak.

As a new planting season begins in most parts of the country, farmers and gardeners carefully place seeds in the rich spring spoil. The nutrients of the soil, water and (pungent) fertilizer release the life within the seed. Roots are established; soon the first stalks and stems break through the ground and into the open air; vines and branches begin to sprout; and, after much careful tilling and pruning, the first fruits and flowers appear.

Part of the miracle is that the fruit of that tiny seed both contains life and sustains life: the harvested crops will provide sustenance to you and me and the rest of creation. And within those fruits are the new seeds that will continue the cycle of life in the next planting season and the next and the next ...

Many metaphors have been employed to depict and explain the Trinity. St. John of Damascus, a great Eastern theologian of the eighth century, said we should think "of the Father as a root, the Son as a branch, and of the Spirit as a fruit, for the sustenance of these three is one." Today's celebration of the Trinity (originating in France in the eighth century and adopted by the universal Church in 1334) focuses on this central understanding of our faith — our belief in the God who has revealed himself as Father, the root that sustains life; Son, the Word of God who grafts us as "branches" to that life; and Spirit, the harvest of God's love in all, binding all, and given to all.

Today's Gospel reading focuses on the relationship between Father and Son and the love (the Spirit) that compels the Father to give his Son for the sake of humanity's salvation. Nicodemus, a Pharisee and member of the Sanhedrin, comes under the cover of darkness to meet the remarkable Rabbi he has heard so much about. In their discussion, Jesus speaks of a God not of endings but beginnings; a God who does not demand the payment of debts but who constantly offers unconditional and unlimited chances to begin again; a God who does not take satisfaction in our failures but rejoices in lifting us up from our brokenness, despair and estrangement from him and from one another.

Humankind realizes its salvation in the loving providence of the Creator who continually invites us back to him; the selfless servanthood of the Redeemer who "emptied" himself to become like us in order that we might become like him; the joyful love of the Spirit that is the unique unity of the Father and Son.

May we behold your presence, O God,
in all its wonders and grace,
in every moment of our lives,
May everything we do give praise to you
as Father:
    the loving Creator and Sustainer of all life;
as Son:
    the Word and Light of God made human for us;
as Spirit:
    the love that binds Father to Son,
    and we to you and to one another.

"I am the living bread that came down from heaven; whoever eats this bread will live forever; and the bread that I will give is my flesh for the life of the world."

John 6: 51–58

"The man who planted trees"

*I*n a short story published a few years after World War II, French writer Jean Giono tells the tale of an old man who lived on a deserted, barren plain between the Alps and Provence. After the death of his wife and son, the old man erected a small cottage for himself and tended a small flock of sheep. Every summer day he would gather as many acorns as he could find. Later that evening, he would examine each one and put aside one hundred perfect acorns. The next day he would go out to a particularly barren place many miles away. He would pound the iron rod he carried into the ground to make a hole and bury an acorn. Every day he planted a hundred acorns. Of those he planted, about a fifth sprouted and grew into magnificent oak trees.

The land was not his; he did not know who owned it nor did he care. His concern was bringing life to this desolate, forgotten place.

Within ten years, his first ten thousand trees were as tall as he was. He began a small nursery of seedlings he had grown from beechnuts; soon beautiful birch trees were taking root in his forest. The wind dispersed seeds, as well.

The old man had planted his trees in valley bottoms where he guessed, correctly, that there was water close to the surface. As the years went by, water began to flow again in stream beds that had been dry for hundreds of years. As the water reappeared, so too did willows, grasses and flowers. Birds and deer and animals of every kind made their home in the new forest. Soon, the long ruined towns nearby were rebuilt by young families drawn to the beauty of the region.

The transformation took place so slowly that nobody noticed. The French government eventually assumed responsibility for the care of the forest, which they believed had come about "naturally."

But it all had sprung up from the hand and vision of this one shepherd who, over four decades, quietly and compassionately transformed this desert into the land of Canaan. It was work worthy of God.

The old shepherd's kindness, humility and patient hope are the very life of God. It is this life that Jesus offers his Church in the sacrament of the Eucharist. Christ calls us not only to consume but to be consumed by the "bread of life" — we become part of the Risen Christ and he becomes part of us. To live in Christ, to feast on the "bread of life," is to look beyond our own self interests and wants and hurts to bring Christ's love, justice and hope into our own barren and desolate forests. In inviting us to feed on his "flesh" and drink of his "blood," we become what we receive: the life that finds joy in humble servanthood to others, the life that is centered in unconditional, total, sacrificial love; the life that seeks fulfillment not in the conventional wisdom of this world but in the holiness of the next.

Today's celebration of the Body and Blood of the Lord originated in the Diocese of Liege in 1246 as the feast of Corpus Christi. In the reforms of Vatican II, Corpus Christi was joined with the feast of the Precious Blood (formerly celebrated on July 1) to become the Solemnity of the Body and Blood of the Lord. We celebrate today Christ's gift of the Eucharist, the source and summit of our life together as the Church.

In the "bread of life" discourse in John's Gospel, Jesus' revelations concerning his Messianic ministry take on a Eucharistic theme. The image of Jesus as "bread from heaven" echoes two dimensions of the same Old Testament image: the wisdom of God's Law nourishing all who accept it and God's blessing of manna to feed the journeying Israelites.

The gift of the Eucharist comes with an important "string" attached: it must be shared. In sharing the body of Christ, we become the body of Christ. If we partake of the "one bread" (Reading 2), then we must be willing to become Eucharist for others — to make the love of Christ real for all. In this sacramental encounter with the Risen One, we are called to become what we have received: to become, in the seedlings and acorns of justice and compassion we plant, Eucharist for one another as Christ is Eucharist for us.

*A*s you give to us, O God, may we give to one another.
May our humble acts of compassion, generosity
    and forgiveness
become visible signs of your invisible grace.
As Christ takes, blesses, breaks and gives his body to us
    in the Eucharist,
may we take, bless, break and give from our own need
    to become Eucharist for others.

ORDINARY TIME

NOTE: The Sundays in this section are numbered according to both the Roman lectionary's designation of Sundays of the Year and the Common lectionary's designation of Sundays after the Epiphany and Propers (Sundays after Pentecost).

Second Sunday of the Year /
Second Sunday after Epiphany

John the Baptist saw Jesus coming toward him and said, "Behold, the Lamb of God, who takes away the sin of the world."

John 1: 29–34

Things will never be the same ...

*L*ate one night, a little boy and his father took the telescope to a field far away from the lights of the city. His dad carefully set up the instrument and positioned the lens. Then Dad had him look down into the eye piece. What the boy saw filled him with awe. He could see the rings of Saturn, the red craters of Mars, and the Sea of Tranquility on Earth's moon. His dad pointed out Polaris, Sirius and the stars of the Big Dipper, Orion and Andromeda. That particular night they could also see the lights of the International Space Station overhead. So began one boy's love of astronomy and fascination with the reaches of outer space. After that night with his dad, he never looked at the stars the same way again.

For years she had listened to the Metropolitan Opera on her radio and watched Met productions on public television. So, for her birthday, her children gave her a trip to New York City and tickets for the Metropolitan's production of Puccini's *Tosca*. With a mixture of excitement and disbelief, she took her seat at Lincoln Center; she was soon transported by the magnificent music and spectacle. Since that magical night at the Met, she now hears music with a joy and insight she never knew before.

He always loved to draw. His sketch book was a kind of retreat, a place that was his alone. One day an artist friend happened to see his sketches. She recognized talent in those pages and encouraged him to develop it. She offered suggestions on technique and style — and he soaked it all up like a sponge. He enrolled in a course in watercolors at the local art institute. His artist friend continued to encourage him and suggested books and exhibits he should see. With a new understanding of form and color, of light and perspective, he sees the world these days with very different eyes.

Today, John the Baptizer invites us to "behold" the Christ, Jesus, the Word of God made flesh, in our midst — and to behold that presence changes everything.

The Fourth Gospel emphasizes John the Baptizer's role as the bridge between the First and New Testaments; he is the last great prophet who identifies Jesus as the Messiah. In his vision of the Spirit of God "resting" upon and within Jesus, the Baptizer realizes that this is the chosen Servant of God who has come to inaugurate the Messianic era of forgiveness and reconciliation (the evangelist John does record the actual baptism of Jesus; in the Fourth Gospel, the Baptizer describes the event and what he saw).

After meeting the Jesus of the Gospels, we will never see the world the same way again; after hearing Jesus' Gospel, peace, forgiveness and justice are possible in ways we could not imagine; after seeing the world through Jesus' eyes, our perspectives and attitudes are transformed in his light. Christ's presence among us is a time for new beginnings: an invitation to walk out of the shadows of hatred and mistrust into the light of understanding and peace, a chance for healing our brokenness and mending our relationships with one another, a call to be seekers of hope and enablers of reconciliation in our own time and place. Through our own acts of compassion and generosity, of justice and forgiveness, we proclaim that "the Lamb of God" walks in our midst, that the love and mercy of God has dawned upon us.

Throughout this new year, the Gospel writers invite us to "behold" the Lamb of God in our midst, transforming our vision, our perspective, our expectations for this life and the life to come. By our baptisms, we are called to be witnesses and prophets of the "Lamb of God" along the Jordan Rivers of our homes, schools and work places.

*L*ord Jesus, Lamb of God,
May we "behold" your presence in our midst
in every moment of this new year and every year.
May your Spirit transform our vision,
our perspective,
our expectations for this life
and the life to come.

Third Sunday of the Year /
Third Sunday after Epiphany

Jesus said to Simon and his brother Andrew, "Come after me, and I will make you fishers of men."

Matthew 4: 12–23

Staying power

A minister was called to the hospital. Caroline, a beautiful baby girl the minister had recently baptized, had been diagnosed with a malignant tumor intertwined with her spinal cord at the base of her brain. Caroline's young parents were stunned with hurt and grief. The minister stayed with the couple throughout the night. But he did not know what to say. *Say something!* he kept telling himself. *A prayer, a verse from Scripture, anything!* But all he could do was cry with the couple.

After some time, a pediatric oncologist came in and outlined a plan to treat the child. The minister was relieved, of course — but he realized that he had nothing to give this family that mattered. Feeling useless, he decided then and there to leave the ministry and do something more important with his life.

Later that night, her parents asked the minister for a favor. "We're exhausted. Caroline won't stop crying. Could you hold her for a little while so we can step out and take a break?"

The minister took Caroline in his arms and rocked her. She cried, and the minister cried, and then having expended all her energy, she drifted off to sleep. The minister kept rocking little Caroline until her parents returned, relieved to see their child at peace. They placed Caroline gently in her crib, and the minister said his goodbyes.

As he stepped into the cold night air, he realized that he would not leave the ministry after all, that all his preparing for ordination and ministry was for this very night: to rock a very sick child to sleep, to offer her and her family whatever little hope he had, to simply love this family in God's name.[1]

The minister discovers one night that his own small net of faith and hope, despite his own doubts about his ability to haul in anything that matters, "catches" a hurting family in the love of God.

In a few lines, Matthew sketches a new beginning in human history: the arrest of John and the end of the First Testament, the beginning of a "New" Testament in the teaching and healing ministry of Jesus in Galilee, and the call of the first disciples from their fishing nets along the Sea of Galilee. Jesus' beginning his public ministry in Galilee is, for Matthew, the fulfillment of an ancient oracle concerning the Messiah: that, through the darkness of Galilee's Assyrian captivity, the "great light" of their deliverance will appear (today's first reading from Isaiah 9). Galilee, unlike the rest of Palestine, had an international perspective; because of its geography and economy, Galilee was influenced by many non-Jewish ideas and perspectives. Josephus, the Roman historian, wrote of the people of Galilee: "They were fond of innovation and, by nature, disposed to change and delighted in sedition ... The Galileans were never destitute of courage ... They were ever more anxious for honor than for gain." The Galilee of Gospel times was the most populated and productive region of Palestine. The great roads of the world passed through Galilee, making it a strategic target for invasion. White-sailed ships crept up the Mediterranean coast from Alexandria and caravans traveled through the region from Mesopotamia and Egypt. In Matthew's account, the ministry of Jesus begins at the shore of the Galilee with a group of itinerant fishermen. Unlike those who followed rabbis and teachers they revered, Jesus calls these fishermen to follow him in a ministry that will demand a radical and total change in their lives.

Christ calls each one of us to be "fishers" of souls using whatever nets we possess, in whatever oceans and seas we navigate. In our own poverty, Christ calls us to "fish" for those who are in need; in our own pain, Christ calls us to "fish" for those who suffer; in our own despair, Christ calls us to "fish" for those who have lost all hope.

*B*e the star by which we navigate our small boats,
Lord Jesus,
as we seek out the lost and forgotten
and bring them safely home.
Guide our hands as we cast our small nets
    into the vast waters,
that we may realize a bounty of hope and grace
as we fish the rough seas of our lives.

Fourth Sunday of the Year /
Fourth Sunday after Epiphany

"Blessed are the poor in spirit, for theirs is the kingdom of heaven ... "

Matthew 5: 1–12

The rich soil of humility

*H*umus is gold to every farmer and gardener. Composed of the decay of plant and animal matter, humus is the most organic and richest part of the soil. When it is tilled and broken open to receive seed and rainfall and sunlight, the dark humus yields the most bountiful harvests and the most beautiful of flowers.

The word *humility* comes from the same root as humus. Like the rich, broken soil of humus, humility is the capacity to be open to receive the seeds of experience — both the painful and the enriching — in order to grow in wisdom and understanding. As the spring soil must be broken of its winter hardness so that it may be enriched by rain and nutrients, humility is the grace to let ourselves be "broken"— broken of our pride, our ego, our self-absorption — in order to realize a harvest far greater than ourselves, a harvest that is possible only through generous openness, selfless giving and enlightened gratitude.

Humility is the grace to plant in hope, persevere through droughts and storms, and reap in joy.

Humility is the growing place of the Beatitudes. To be a people of the Beatitudes is to embrace the spirit of humility that begins with valuing life as a gift from God, a gift we have received only through God's mysterious love, not through anything we have done to deserve it. Jesus calls all who would be his disciples to embrace the "blessedness" of the Sermon on the Mount: to "detach" from material things in order to "attach" ourselves to the things of God; to realize our need to be forgiven and reconciled with God and family and friends; to embrace the spirit of "mercy" that enables us to consider things from the perspective of others and feel their joys and sorrows; to be makers of "peace" that honors and upholds humanity's highest good.

The word "blessed," as used by Jesus in these eight maxims, is written in Greek as *makarios*, a word which indicates a joy that is God-like in its serenity and totality.

Specific Greek words used throughout the text indicate several important meanings:

"The poor in spirit": those who are detached from material things, who put their trust in God.

"The sorrowing": this Beatitude speaks of the value of caring and compassion — the hallmarks of Jesus' teaching.

"The lowly": the Greek word used here is *praotes* — true humility that banishes all pride; the lowly are the "blessed" who accept the necessity to learn and grow and realize their need to be forgiven.

"They who show mercy": the Greek word *chesedh* used here indicates the ability to get "inside a person's skin" to see things from his/her perspective, consider things from his/her experience mind and feel his/her joys and sorrows.

"The peacemakers": peace is not merely the absence of trouble or discord but peace is a positive condition: it is everything that provides and makes for humanity's highest good; note, too, that the "blessed" are described as peace-*makers* and not simply peace-*lovers.*

The "blessed" of the Gospel have embraced a spirit of humble gratitude before the God who gives, nurtures and sustains our lives. The "blessed" seek to respond to such unfathomable love the only way they can: by returning that love to others, God's children, as a way of returning it to God. As a people of faith we are called to focus our lives on the "blessedness" of the Sermon on the Mount: to seek our joy and fulfillment in God above all things. Our "blessedness" cannot be measured by our portfolios, celebrity or intellect, but in our ability to grasp that we exist not in and of ourselves but by and in the love of God.

Gracious God,
make us a people of the beatitudes —
may we discover the "blessed" happiness
of being detached from material things;
of embracing your Word of comfort in the face
    of life's difficulties;
of finding joy and purpose in service to others;
of seeking what is just and right in all things;
of becoming vessels of your mercy and forgiveness
    for all;
of listening to you speak to us in the quiet of hearts;
of working for peace in our homes and communities;
of taking up our own crosses as your Son took up his
for the sake of justice and righteousness;
of spending all that we have and are to establish
    your kingdom
in our own time and place.

"You are the salt of the earth. But if salt loses its taste, with what can it be seasoned … ?
"You are the light of the world. A city set on a mountain cannot be hidden … "

Matthew 5: 13–16
[Roman lectionary]

Matthew 5: 13–20
[Common lectionary]

Humble salt, generous light

*E*ver eat a handful of salt? Or drink a glass of ocean water?

Of course not. Salt by itself does not taste particularly good — it might even make you sick to your stomach.

Ever look directly at the sun or into a bright, burning bulb?

Not without doing permanent damage to your eyes.

Salt and sun, of themselves, are not good for very much and can even be harmful. Their value is realized only when they mix or interact with other things. Their addition brings out the fullness of whatever they come in contact with.

That handful of salt, acrid tasting of itself, can bring out the natural flavor in every kind of food, from filet to popcorn. The four ounces of salt in our bodies enable our muscles to contract, our blood to circulate, our hearts to beat. Salt purifies and softens, cleans and preserves. Salt is an important element in making glass, building roads, manufacturing soap and shampoo, bleaching paper and cooling nuclear reactors. Salt is used both in freezing and in de-icing. There are over 14,000 uses of salt — but by itself, salt is useless.

Light's true beauty is realized only when we look away from its source and toward what it illuminates. Light transforms the cold terror of night into the warm assurance of day. Light enables us to discover, to study, to discern, to behold the beauty of our world and the wonders of God's creation. Light warms, nurtures, sustains, reveals, cheers.

Salt is perhaps the most humble of all chemicals; light is among the most generous of all physical properties.

In calling us to become salt and light for the earth, Jesus asks us to embrace that same humility and generosity. Those who are "salt of the earth" are not just those who are virtuous themselves but who bring out the goodness in us and everyone else. Those who are a "light for the world" divert attention from themselves in order to illuminate the goodness of God in our midst. To become "salt" in the spirit of Christ is to bring forth the "flavor" of God in everyone and everything; to be "light" that is a reflection of Christ is to illuminate the presence of God in the midst of the dark and the cold, the hidden and the unclear.

Through the images of salt and light in Matthew's Gospel, Jesus impresses upon his listeners the vocation of the disciple: *As I am salt and light to the world, so you, as my disciples, must reflect me to the world.*

The reading in the Common lectionary continues Jesus' discourse, with Jesus making a clear connection between the Law of ancient Israel and the promises it holds and the Gospel of compassion and justice he comes now to proclaim. He assures his first hearers that he comes not to change or destroy but to fulfill. Jesus' call for "righteousness [that] surpasses that of the scribes and Pharisees" is a theme that echoes throughout Matthew's Gospel: that Jesus' Gospel requires a conversion of heart rather than a spiritless adherence to legalities and traditions. *[For more, see the essay for next Sunday.]*

O God,
make us your salt for the earth —
that, in our own humble, hidden acts
    of generosity and peace
we may reveal your love in the midst of us all;
make us your light for the world —
that we may reflect your compassion and forgiveness
the light and warmth of your love
in the midst of cold, dark winter;
make us your city on the hill —
the vision of your dream of a world
united in your justice and mercy.

Sixth Sunday of the Year /
Sixth Sunday after Epiphany

"Do not think I have come to abolish the law or the prophets. Amen, I say to you, I have come not to abolish but to fulfill ... You have heard it said to your ancestors, 'You shall not kill; and whoever kills will be liable to judgment.' But I say to you, Whoever is angry with his brother will be liable to judgment ... "

Matthew 5: 17–37

The Road

Cormac McCarthy's Pulitzer-Prize winning novel *The Road* is the dark, compelling story of a father and son fighting for survival in the midst of nuclear winter.

Nuclear war has reduced America to ashes. Millions have been killed; cities and countrysides have been destroyed. The few people who survived the firestorm have banded into marauding packs robbing and killing for food.

A man in his late forties and his ten-year-old son who managed to survive are making their way from the eternal winter in the north to the southern coast where, they hope, they will find warmth and some chance of building a life. The boy, who was born after the war, has no memory of the better, happier times his father has known. Every day of their trek, the father keeps reminding the son that they are the "good guys" who carry the "fire." The boy is never quite sure exactly what the "fire" is — but he believes in the "fire" because his father has told him so, and that's good enough for him.

Throughout their journey along *The Road,* the boy displays heartbreaking compassion for everyone they encounter — even those who try to kill them for their meager provisions. Along the dark, gray *Road,* father and son confront starvation, bitter cold, sickness, horror and death. At the end of the journey, when his father finally succumbs to illness and exhaustion, the boy must take to *The Road* himself, and he begins to understand what the "fire" is — his father's uncompromising, unconditional love for his son that enabled him to survive.

"Do everything the way we did," his father tells his son, and remember that the fire "is inside you. It was always there. I can see it."

The boy continues on *The Road* with that hope.

Christ calls us, in today's Gospel, to pass on the "fire" — the love of God for all his sons and daughters, the hope of transforming the darkness and bitterness of our world into the kingdom of God, the peace that enables all men and women to live as brothers and sisters in God's Christ. By our compassion and caring for others, by our ethical and moral convictions, by our sense of awareness and gratitude for all that God has done for us, we do the great work of passing on the "fire" of the Gospel of compassion and justice.

That "fire" of compassion collides with technicalities of law in today's Gospel, the first indication of trouble between Jesus and the leaders of the Jews. Over time, the role of the scribes evolved from being the recorders and codifiers of the Torah into that of interpreters of the specific rules and regulations of the Torah. The Pharisees, the "separated brethren," removed themselves from everyday activity in order to keep the Law assiduously, thereby serving as a model to the Jewish people who held them in great esteem.

While the scribes and Pharisees were obsessed with the meticulous keeping of the letter of the Law, Jesus taught the importance of the more difficult task of embracing the Spirit of God, the attitude of love and humility that endows all just laws with their life and meaning. We often approach laws and rules as the minimum required of us — beyond what is specifically defined and clearly spelled out, anything goes.

But for Jesus, the human heart is decisive in determining what is right and wrong. Our faithfulness to prayer and worship means nothing if hatred and selfishness separate us from family and friends; anger is more than an emotion but the beginning of a potentially destructive chain of events in human relationships; promiscuity and unfaithfulness cannot be dismissed as mere "failings" but must be seen as an unacceptable degrading of men and women.

Christ speaks not of rules and regulations but of the most profound values of the human heart. "What else are the laws of God," St. Augustine said, "but the very presence of the Holy Spirit."

*L*ord Jesus, inspire us with the "fire" of your love
so that we may, in turn, pass on that "fire" to others.
Bless our efforts to reflect the light and warmth
    of that fire
in our homes and workplaces, our classrooms and
    playgrounds.
Open our hearts and consciences
to behold your Spirit of justice and compassion
written in every just law
and celebrated in every ritual and tradition.

"You have heard that it was said, 'You shall love your neighbor and hate your enemy.' But I say to you, Love your enemies, and pray for those who persecute you … For if you love those who love you, what recompense will you have?"

Matthew 5: 38–48

The hard work of hating

In Lynn Johnson's wonderful daily comic strip about the simple joys and travails of family life, *For Better or For Worse*, teenager Lizzy has had a fight with her friend Candace over a boy. The two are not speaking. In the first panel, Lizzy and Candace walk right by each other. "There's Candace," Lizzy says to herself. "I do not know her."

Second panel, in the corridor, on the way to class: "She's going down the hall one way, so I'll go the other way. If she sits near me in class, I'll move!!"

Third panel, in class: "Here comes Candace. If she talks to me, I'll pretend I didn't hear her. If she looks at me, I'll pretend I didn't see her."

In the final panel, with Candace sitting in the background, Lizzy puts her head in her hands and realizes, "Whew! I didn't think hating somebody could be so much WORK!"[2]

It's true, isn't it? To really *hate* someone demands a great deal of wasted time, energy and emotion. But God's gift of life is not meant to be squandered on estrangement and alienation but to be celebrated in the love of family and friends.

The challenge of the Gospel is to be ready and willing to take that first difficult step towards forgiving and seeking forgiveness; to refuse to allow bitterness to close our hearts to someone, regardless of how deeply they hurt us; to put aside our own need for the justice "due" us for the good of others.

In today's Gospel, Jesus continues to take the Law beyond the boundaries, formulas and measurements of its official arbiters. Of course, nowhere in the New Testament does the phrase "hate your enemy" appear — the concept of "enemy" was an assumption on the part of the scribes and Pharisees, who defined an enemy as anyone not a Jew. But Jesus challenges that assumption: God's love unites all men and women, on whom the Father's "sun rises and sets as well." However justified retaliation might appear to be, Jesus calls us to seek reconciliation instead of vengeance.

In the Greek text of Matthew's Gospel, the word used in today's text for love is *agape.* The word indicates not a romantic or emotional kind of love we have for the special ones in our lives but, rather, a state of benevolence and good will. The love that Jesus asks us to have for our "enemies" means that no matter how he/she hurts us, we will never let bitterness close our hearts to that person nor will we seek anything but good for that "enemy." Agape begins with recognizing the humanity we share with all people who call God "Father." God's reign of justice and peace can only be realized when individuals freely surrender their own interests, needs and "just" due for the good of others.

Christ calls us to be a people of "agape": to love the unlovable, to reach out to the alienated, to dismantle whatever walls divide and isolate people and build bridges that bring people together. As Lizzy discovers with Candace — and as we all know, even though we are reluctant to admit it — this life God has given each one of us is too precious, too short, to waste on anything less than the love of God its Giver. We all know someone from whom we are estranged, individuals we can't stand, people we would rather have nothing to do with. Isn't there an avenue we can take, an opening we can explore, a hand we can extend to heal wounds and mend bridges between us and them?

Not to do so is such a waste of time and energy.

After all, there are so many better things to do than to waste time and energy on hating.

It's too much work.

*L*ord, may the light of your wisdom enable us
to recognize our role in the endless cycle
of tension, distrust, anger and war
that destroys our world.
Transform our hearts that we may take on
the work of forgiveness —
the work that heals and transforms.
May your Son's spirit of humility and love
move our spirits to be ready to love first,
despite the cost.

Sunday 8 / Proper 3

"Look at the birds in the sky; they do not sow or reap, they gather nothing into barns, yet your heavenly Father feeds them. Are you not more important than they? Can any of you by worrying add a single moment to your life-span ... ? But seek first the kingdom of God and his righteousness, and all these things will be given you besides."

Matthew 6: 24–34

Sands of time

*I*magine spending hours creating a beautiful work of art — and then, as a prayer, destroying it.

That is the ritual performed in many Tibetan monasteries to introduce students to the principles of Buddhism. Over a nine-day period, with prayers and chanting, the monks create an elaborate and beautiful sand painting, called a *mandala*. The painting, seven feet in diameter, is composed of colored sand, chalk, saffron spice and wheat. The finished *mandala* includes representations of all the sacred principles of Buddhism. The monks pray that the Divine will descend from the heavens and temporarily "live" in the *mandala*. When the *mandala* is completed, students are then invited to come and study with the monks the meaning of the various symbols and signs and, through the *mandala,* be reborn in the faith.

In the final part of the ritual, the monks offer thanks for the divine presence in their work and request that God "leave" the *mandala*. Then the sands of the *mandala* are ritually defaced and placed in urns. The monks solemnly take the urns to a nearby lake or river and prayerfully pour the sands into the waters. Like the passing of all things, the *mandala* is washed away, existing forever in the memories of those who created it and those who discovered God in it.

We carry on everyday believing that we are building a life, a legacy, a world that will last forever. But everything we possess or create or use is like the sands of the monks' painting — some day, sooner rather than later, it will all be washed away. Today's Gospel calls us to let go of the things that fill our lives and, instead, seek to possess the lasting treasures of God: love of family and friends, the sense of meaning that comes from living the principles of justice and mercy, the joy of helping others realize their dreams and hopes for themselves and their families.

In the Gospels, Jesus condemns neither work nor possessions, but he places them in perspective. Material wealth is, rightly, a tool we use to cooperate with God in the work of completing creation; but whatever things become barriers between our lives and the life of God are idols to be rejected. Jesus' admonition on serving "two masters" and the parables of the birds and wild flowers challenge our scale of values: Do we exist to acquire the holiness of God or the riches of life? Jesus does not deny the reality of basic human needs for food and clothing, but to displace the holiness of God with the perishables of wealth and power is the ultimate human tragedy.

O God, you are the Source of all blessings
and Author of all that is good.
Open our hearts to your grace
so that we may open our hands
to let go of the "sand" that we fill our hours with
at the expense of your life and love.
May we see everything we consume and own,
everything that warms us and protects us
as signs of your providence.

"Not everyone who says to me, 'Lord, Lord,' will enter the kingdom of heaven, but only the one who does the will of my Father in heaven ... Everyone who hears these words of mine and acts on them will be like the wise man who built his house on rock ... "

Matthew 7: 21–27

Lost and found

*W*riter Sue Norton, in an essay in *Commonweal* magazine, recounts the weekend she and her husband celebrated their wedding anniversary in Paris.

It was a cold weekend — and it wasn't the weather. *She* thought the weekend would be an opportunity to reflect on their marriage; *he* was going for the fine food, the wine, the sights. She wanted to talk; he wanted a break. She sought enlightenment; he looked forward to the "city of lights." They barely had their first croissant before they were at odds.

One evening, after a particularly expensive and painfully silent dinner, they were walking back to their hotel when she spotted a leather wallet on the ground. Inside the wallet were tattered family photos, a small silver cross, a personal letter in Spanish — and a weekly appointment card for psychiatric care and a current identity card for a shelter run by the St. Vincent de Paul Society. They spent most of their last day in Paris trying to return the wallet to its owner, putting aside their impatience and disappointment to find the shelter. Late that afternoon, they found the shelter on a narrow Paris street — it was closed. Across the street was a small hotel. A sympathetic desk clerk agreed to take the wallet and return it.

As they boarded their flight for home the following day, she realized that they had both gotten what they wanted from their Paris weekend:

"We had spoken so little, both before and after the wallet incident. But despite our silence, we located our common ground. Neither of us had asked the other, Should we try to return the wallet? Neither of us asked the other if we should stop trying to return it. We had both understood that we had to return it, and so we did. We may have lost an important weekend, but in a way that I suspected would sustain us for a long time to come, we found ourselves …

"The plane lifted off, looped around the Eiffel Tower, and set off in the direction home. I reached out my hand and he took it."[3]

In the midst of their "stormy" anniversary in Paris, this couple discovered that their life together was built on the "rock" of compassion and generosity, of kindness and selflessness. In today's Gospel, Jesus concludes the Sermon on the Mount by exhorting his listeners to put the words of the Gospel into action. The faith we actually *live* is the faith we really believe. One's sincerity is reflected in one's deeds; words can never substitute for actions.

Real faith is centered in the values of the heart, with an understanding of God's love for us and the irrepressible longing to respond to that love. The Gospel challenges us to bridge the chasm that often exists between what we say we believe and the values we actually live and practice. The faithful disciple understands that the love of God is the center of all things and seeks to bring that love, with conviction, integrity and perseverance, into his/her life and the lives of others.

O God, be the rock on which we build our lives.
Open our hearts and spirits to hear you
in the voices of one another.
Help us to confront the pain and hurt
our selfishness causes those we love

and to understand how our failure to love and forgive
destroys the houses we have built for our families.
By your wisdom and grace,
may we realize that we are never alone,
that in life's most destructive storms
you are with us in the love and forgiveness of family
    and friends.

Jesus saw a man named Matthew sitting at a customs post. He said to him, "Follow me … "
"Go and learn the meaning of the words, 'I desire mercy, not sacrifice.' "

Matthew 9: 9–13
[Roman lectionary]

Matthew 9: 9–13, 18–26
[Common lectionary]

At this altar

*E*very week we gather around this altar. We place on it bread and wine and offer them to God; God returns them to us as the body and blood of his Beloved Son.

But imagine for a moment a bigger altar, an altar on which is placed not just the Eucharistic elements, but the elements of mercy, compassion, justice, forgiveness.

Place on the altar your favorite casserole dish, the one you use to prepare suppers for neighbors experiencing crisis or hardship. Place on the altar the alphabet book you read every night with your child, during those special moments of quiet grace. Include in your offering the stuff of family life: the keys to the family van, the basketball you and your kids shoot hoops with, the portfolio that will fund their college education.

Place on the altar the watch you put aside when a friend needs to talk … the yarn you use to knit shawls for the parish Prayer Shawl ministry … the return envelope that holds the donations you solicit from neighbors for charity.

With the Eucharist, we offer our means of mercy, our tools of reconciliation, our humble efforts to heal and reconcile. God accepts them and returns them as grace, blessing and hope. They are sacramental; they are Eucharistic; they are God in our midst.

In today's Gospel, Jesus repeats the words of Psalm 51: God seeks no greater gift from us than our extending his mercy to others. Mercy — to extend love, peace, compassion, forgiveness and support to those who have done nothing to deserve them — is the cutting edge of the Gospel.

Jesus' "foil" for his lesson on mercy is a tax collector named Matthew, whom Jesus has just called to join his circle. That Jesus would even speak to a tax collector raises eyebrows among his Jewish hearers. Tax collectors like Matthew were despised by the Jews. Matthew's profession was considered corrupt and a betrayal of Judaism. And there was good reason for this antipathy.

Realizing it could never efficiently collect taxes from every subject in its far-flung empire, the Roman government auctioned off the right to collect taxes in a given area. Whoever bought that right was responsible to the Roman government for the agreed upon amount; whatever the purchaser could collect over and above that sum was his commission. How he "collected" those taxes was of little concern to the Romans. It was a system that effectively legalized corruption, extortion and bribery. The Jews considered tax collectors (also known as publicans) collaborators with their nation's occupiers who became wealthy men by taking advantage of their people's misfortune.

Jesus' including a tax collector in his closest circle, as well as welcoming known sinners into his company, scandalized the Pharisees. Citing the words of the prophet Hosea (today's first reading), Jesus states unequivocally that his Messianic mission is universal in nature and spirit and not limited to the coldly orthodox and piously self-righteous of Israel. Christ comes to call all men and women — Jew and Gentile, rich and poor, saint and sinner — back to the Father. Because of their concern with criticism instead of encouragement and condemnation instead of forgiveness, the Pharisees (the self-proclaimed "separated ones") fail to understand that God speaks directly, not through legal proscriptions and impersonal theological treatises, but through compassion and reconciliation to all human hearts.

In citing Psalm 51 ("I desire mercy, not sacrifice"), Christ demands of us, if we are to be his disciples, to make our churches, homes, schools and communities places of welcome and harbors of mercy for all. Our worship means very little if we are conscious of our faith only for this one hour each week — our praise of God should reflect and celebrate the joy and love we live every day of every week; otherwise, as Hosea says, our worship is "like the dew that early passes away."

So let us make room on our parish altar/table for not just the bread and wine of the Eucharist but the elements we use to make God's loving presence real in our homes and communities.

In the Common lectionary, today's Gospel continues with Matthew's account of Jesus' curing of the twelve-year-old daughter of an "official" (Matthew gives no other description of the father) and the woman who has suffered from hemorrhages for 12 years. Matthew's story parallels the story of Jairus' daughter in Mark 5: 21–43, though Matthew has left out many of the details included in Mark's account (Matthew does include two details that would resonate with his Jewish audience: the flute players prescribed for Jewish funerals and the "tassels" on Jesus' cloak, worn by all Jewish men as talismans of God's commandments). The two healing stories exalt the faith of the anguished father and the suffering woman.

Both stories in today's Gospel — Matthew's call and the healing of the young girl and the woman with hemorrhages — focus on the reality that faith begins with realizing that we deserve nothing from God, not even the gift of life itself. All that we are and have are the blessings of a God whose profound and unimaginably limitless love has compelled God to create, nurture and bless us.

*A*ccept, O Lord, the prayers we offer at this table:
the sacrifices we joyfully make for those we love,
the offering of our humble works of justice and mercy,

the benediction of the generosity and forgiveness
we are able to extend
and our brothers and sisters extend to us.
Hear these prayers we offer —
prayers you inspire us to make,
prayers that by your grace we are able to realize
in our time and place.

At the sight of the crowds, Jesus' heart was moved with pity for them because they were like sheep without a shepherd. Jesus sent out [the] twelve after instructing them thus, "Cure the sick, raise the dead, cleanse lepers, drive out demons. Without cost you have received; without cost you are to give."

Matthew 9: 36–10: 8

"Being there"

A minister took up a new parish among one of the poorest and crime-ridden areas of the city. When he first moved into the neighborhood, the minister sought out a local drug dealer and gang leader named Selvin, who took the reverend to crack houses and gang hangouts. Selvin gave his guest an important lesson in why God was losing to gangs in the battle for the souls of inner-city kids:

"I'm there when Johnny goes out for a loaf of bread for Mama. I'm here and you're not. I win, you lose. It's all about being there."[4]

Jesus' missionary call is all about "being there" — "being there" for the sick, the weak and needy, the helplessly and hopelessly "dead," the alienated, the rejected and the abused — the people we would prefer having nothing to do with.

Today's Gospel serves as a narrative transition from Matthew's recounting of Jesus' miraculous deeds (chapters 8 and 9) to Jesus' missionary discourse (chapters 10 and 11). The missionary dimension of discipleship is underscored by two images: the people who are "like sheep without a shepherd" and the need for laborers to gather the harvest. Having established his authority as a healer, Jesus now passes on to the Twelve the "gift" of their own call and mission to the people of Israel (the number *twelve* is highly symbolic here, representing the twelve tribes of Israel:

the apostles' mission is to the new Israel, whose tribes encompass all nations and peoples).

We are surrounded by all kinds of experts, leaders and gurus who admonish and advise us on how to feel better about ourselves and how to cope with the struggle and dysfunction that are part of every life; but Jesus' compassion for the "shepherdless" confronts us with our yearning for authentic guides who show us not merely how to feel good but how to transform our sadness into joy and our despair into hope, who lead us beyond coping to conversion, who inspire us not just to happiness but to compassion, justice and reconciliation. Out of that concern, Jesus commissions the Twelve to make the same proclamation of salvation as Jesus (Matthew 4: 17) and John the Baptizer (Matthew 3: 2). He also sends them forth to heal — not just physical healing, but to heal hearts and souls in a ministry of reconciliation:

- *"cure the sick"*: bring back to God those who are alienated, those who are weak in faith (the word used in the Greek text *asthenes* means "weak");
- *"raise the dead"*: bring back those hopelessly and helplessly dead because of sin and blind and deaf to the goodness of the love of God;
- *"heal the leprous"*: bring back those who have been rejected or are separated from God's people;
- *"expel demons"*: liberate those enslaved by sin and evil.

As shepherds to his people, as teachers of his Gospel, as healers and vehicles of reconciliation, Jesus sends forth the Twelve — and all of us — to *be there* for others. We and every Christian are called to be the human face of Christ in our own time and place: to *be there* with compassion, forgiveness and understanding for those who journey outside our own comfortable orbit; to *be there* to help the lost and fallen rebuild their lives; to *be there* to heal and repair broken relationships.

*B*y your grace, O Lord,
may we "be there" for one another:
May we "be there" for the sick and the dying,
for those labeled as "lepers" and "demons,"
for the troubled, the lost, the ridiculed,
for the alienated and the forgotten.
Let us give to others as you have given to us;
let us forgive one another as you have forgiven us;
let us be peace for all as you are our peace.

Sunday 12 / Proper 7

" ... Do not be afraid; you are worth more than many sparrows ... Everyone who acknowledges me before others I will acknowledge before my heavenly Father."

Matthew 10: 26–33
[Roman lectionary]

Matthew 10: 24–39
[Common lectionary]

Drive on ...

*O*ne cold February afternoon, a young doctor, still in residency, was driving behind a Bronco SUV that suddenly slammed into a pickup truck. While the driver of the Bronco was not hurt, the driver of the pickup was trapped in his vehicle. He was unconscious and not breathing — and reeking of alcohol. The doctor knew he had to do something to open the man's air passage or he would die — but, without knowing the extent of the man's neck injuries, to move him could result in paralyzing him. Aware that he risked a lawsuit that could end his career, the doctor decided to save the drunk driver's life. The man survived and fully recovered.

A few days later, the resident told one of his senior professors the story. The professor peered over his glasses and his eyes narrowed. "Well, you did the right thing medically of course. But, James, do you know what you put at risk by doing that?" he said sternly.

"What was I supposed to do?" the young doctor asked.

"Drive on," his professor replied. "There is an army of lawyers out there who would stand in line to get a case like that. If that driver had turned out to be a quadriplegic, you might never have practiced medicine again. You were a very lucky man."

The young doctor, now practicing rehabilitation medicine in New York, reflects:

"The day I graduated from medical school, I took an oath to serve the sick and injured. I remember truly believing I would be able to do just that. But I have found out it isn't so simple. I understand now what a foolish thing I did that day. Despite my oath, I know what I would do on that cold roadside near Gettysburg today. I would drive on."[5]

While our hearts and spirits yearn to do what is right and good, any number of circumstances compels us to think twice about the consequences of our involvement — and then to shrug our shoulders and walk away. Three times in today's Gospel, however, Jesus tells his disciples not to be afraid, that we have nothing to fear before God who has proven his love and acceptance of us unreservedly. Fear is most destructive when it chokes us off from creating or accomplishing what is right, just and good — but the realization that we have nothing to fear from any person, group or institution is the ultimate liberation and empowerment. In "fearing" nothing but God and concerned only in seeking God's will in all things do we become faithful disciples of the Gospel Jesus.

In Matthew's missionary discourse, Jesus instills in his disciples the need for openness and courage in their preaching of the Gospel. The disciple who faithfully proclaims the Gospel will likely be denounced, ridiculed and abused; but Jesus assures his followers that they have nothing to fear from those who can deprive "the body of life," for their perseverance and courage in proclaiming the Gospel of Jesus will be rewarded in the reign of God.

*L*et us walk always in the light of your peace,
Confident of your love and grace, O God of compassion.
May selfishness not eclipse your presence in our midst;
may fear not blind us to your image
in the faces of all our brothers and sisters;
may despair not shatter our hope in your providence.

Sunday 13 / Proper 8

"Whoever loves father or mother more than me is not worthy of me ... and whoever does not take up his cross and follow me is not worthy of me ... And whoever gives only a cup of cold water to one of these little ones to drink because the little one is a disciple — amen, I say to you, he will surely not lose his reward."

Matthew 10: 37–42

The cost of the corner office

*T*he company threw a lavish dinner to honor its CEO upon his retirement. His rise to the executive suite was meteoric; his management of the company, through tough times and boom times, had been masterful; everything he touched, it seemed, turned to gold. He had made himself and the company's senior managers and stockholders very wealthy people.

At the retirement dinner, the CEO addressed his remarks to the company's young executives:

"I know you all want my job. Let me tell you how to get it. Last week my daughter was married, and as I walked her down the aisle, I realized I did not know the name of her best friend, or the last book she read, or her favorite color. That's the price I paid for this job. If you want to pay that price, you can have it."

Sometimes it takes an accounting of what we possess to discover what we lack; in confronting the extent of our wealth we realize own poverty. Jesus' words today are echoed in the CEO's pitiable valedictory to his young executives: We can become so absorbed with building a career that we fail to develop our full potential and talents as human beings; we can become so obsessed with creating and maintaining a lifestyle that we fail to live a life worth living. Christ calls all who would be his disciples to "lose" life's obsessive, meaningless and petty pursuits in order to "find" a life fully human and alive in hope and joy.

Today's Gospel is the conclusion of Matthew's collection of Jesus' missionary counsels. Jesus speaks of the sacrifice demanded of his disciples and the suffering they will endure for their faith. Though his words may sound harsh, Jesus is not attacking family life here; Jesus' call to discipleship demands a complete commitment to his mission of reconciliation and peace, putting aside whatever compromises or distracts us from that call.

Jesus is also warning his disciples of the conflict and misunderstanding they will experience for proclaiming his Gospel. To be an authentic disciple of Jesus means embracing the suffering, humility, pain and selflessness of the cross; to be an authentic disciple of Jesus means taking on the often-unpopular role of prophet for the sake of the kingdom; to be an authentic disciple of Jesus means welcoming and supporting other disciples who do the work of the Gospel.

To "receive the prophet's reward" is to seek out every opportunity, to use every talent with which we have been blessed, to devote every resource at our disposal to make the love of God a living reality in every life we touch. God calls every one of us to the work of the *prophet* — to proclaim his presence among his people. Some are called to be witnesses of God's justice in the midst of profound evil; others are called to be witnesses of his hope to those in pain and anguish; and many share in the work of the prophet/witness by enabling others to be effective witnesses and ministers of God's love. The gift of faith opens our spirits to realize and accept our call to be witnesses of God's love borne on the cross and prophets of the hope of his Son's resurrection.

*L*ord Jesus, the very Light of God,
illuminate our minds and hearts to behold your presence
in the love of family and friends,
to perceive your path of holiness and justice
in our journey through time,
to take up our crosses in the knowledge that,
by your grace,
we can make them vehicles of resurrection
in this time and place of ours.

Sunday 14 / Proper 9

" ... although you have hidden these things from the wise and the learned you have revealed them to little ones ... "Come to me, all you who labor and are burdened, and I will give you rest. Take my yoke upon you and learn from me, for I am meek and humble of heart ... "

Matthew 11: 25–30
[Roman lectionary]

Matthew 11: 16–19, 25–30
[Common lectionary]

The book of Gospels

*O*ne of the "saints" of Zen Buddhism is a priest named Tetsugen, who was the first to translate the holy books of his faith into Japanese.

The priest sought to print several thousand copies of the books in order to make the texts of Japan's religion available to everyone. He traveled the length and breadth of Japan to raise the money for the printing. Rich and poor alike donated to the project. The priest expressed equal gratitude to each donor, whether their gift amounted to hundreds of pieces of gold or a few pennies.

After ten long years, Tetsugen had enough money for the printing. But just as the making of the holy books was about to begin, the river Uji overflowed its banks. The disaster left thousands of people without food and shelter. The priest halted the project immediately and used all of the money he worked so hard to raise to help the hungry and homeless.

Once the crisis eased, Tetsugen went to work raising the funds all over again. It took another ten years of travel and begging before he collected the money he needed for the engraving and printing of the holy book. But an epidemic spread across the country. Again the priest gave away all he had collected for the sick, the suffering and dying.

A third time Tetsugen set out on his travels and, twenty years later, his dream of having the wisdom of his faith printed in Japanese was finally realized.

The printing blocks that produced the first edition are on display at the Obaku Monastery in Kyoto. The Japanese tell their children that Tetsugen actually published three editions of the holy book: the first two are invisible but far superior to the third.

Tetsugen's selflessness proved to be a more effective proclamation of his faith than the words of faith he dreamed to print. Love as a living, creative expression of faith is the heart of today's Gospel.

Rarely outside of John's Gospel is Jesus' intimacy with God so clearly portrayed as in today's Gospel from Matthew. Jesus offers a hymn of praise to his Father, the holy Creator of all who deeply loves his creation as a father loves his children. The great love of God for all of humanity is revealed in the love of his Son, the Messiah.

Religion as a "yoke" was exactly how Jesus' Jewish listeners understood the Law. They saw their faith as a burden, a submission to a set of endless rules and regulations dictating every dimension of their lives. But Jesus describes *his* "yoke" as "easy." The Greek word used here that we translate as "easy" more accurately means "fitting well." In Palestine, ox yokes were custom-made of wood, cut and measured to fit a particular animal. Jesus proposes here a radical change in attitude regarding faith: Our relationship with God is not based on how meticulously we keep a certain set of rules and regulations (a direct challenge to the long-held view of the scribes and Pharisees) but in the depth of our love of God, reflected in our love of others.

In calling us to be "gentle" and "humble of heart," Jesus does not call us to be simpletons or anti-intellectuals nor should faith be "dumbed down." Jesus calls us to embrace God's spirit of love and compassion — love that is not compromised by self-interest and rationalization, compassion that is offered totally and unreservedly, completely, without limit or condition.

[There is also an important political dimension to today's pericope, as well. Matthew's Gospel was written a short time after the destruction of Jerusalem in the year 70 A.D. by the soldier-emperor Vespasian. For both the established Jewish communities and the fledgling Christian churches, it was a time of painful introspection: Would Israel's hope for the political restoration of the Jewish state ever be realized? While orthodox Jews maintained unwavering fidelity to their people, language and sense of nationalism, the Christian "cult" saw their ultimate destiny not in the political restoration of Israel but in the coming of the reign of God, a reign that embraces not just Jews but all men and women — even Israel's most despised enemies. Jewish suspicion of the Christian community was growing as the new group became more and more disaffected by the Jewish political agenda. Jesus' words on gentleness and humility set off sparks between loyal Jews and Christians who were abandoning the cause.]

Jesus invites us to embrace the joyful sense of fulfillment that can only be realized by "learning" from his example of humility and gratitude, to take on his "yoke" of humble, joyful service to one another as we journey together to the dwelling place of God. Like Tetsugen, we proclaim the Gospel most effectively and meaningfully not in words but in the generosity and compassion we extend to others. In our work for justice, in our dedication to reconciliation, in our welcome to all who approach our tables, we make the word of God a living reality in our own time and place.

Every parent and teacher can identify with Jesus' lament over the fickleness of the younger generation (Matthew 11: 16–19, which opens today's Gospel reading in the Common lectionary). Children are exasperating. They live for the moment; they become bored in an instant. More often than not, they have no idea what they want — but are clear about what they *don't* want. Whatever they have, they want something else. They bristle at limits and chafe at rules but are not mature enough to know how to function without them. The child has the innate ability to cajole, to negotiate, to make you feel horrible for *daring* to say no.

The truth is we adults are often like children in our relationship with God. We want God to do this and mean this one day, then be something entirely different the next minute: *Forgive us*

our failings, O God — but punish those who hurt us. Bless us —
but don't let that other guy get more than us. If I'm good today, O
God, can I get tomorrow off?

In the short parable that opens the Gospel pericope, Jesus admonishes those whose faith seems to be stuck in childishness. Like sullen, persnickety children, "this generation" rejects the austerity of John, but at the same time rejects the openness of Jesus. They find fault with both the "dirge" of repentance played by John and the "flute" of joy played by Jesus. They refuse to play either the "happy" games of Jesus or the "serious" games of John.

Wisdom demands a mature approach to God and the things of God. A maturity of faith is centered in the realization that we are not the center of the universe, that there exists outside of ourselves that sacred entity that breathes life into our beings and animates all of creation. To become an "adult" man and woman of faith begins with gratitude for the gift of life that is of and from God. The love of God starts with the realization of the needs of another, putting our own wants second. Christ calls us to a *childlike* faith of simplicity and humility, not a *childish* faith of "even-Stevens" and "me-firsts."

*O*pen our hearts, O God,
to embrace your Spirit
that created and continues to animate all of creation.
Grateful for your gift of life
and humbled before your inexplicable love for us,
may we be worthy to be your sons and daughters.

Sunday 15 / Proper 10

The parable of the sower: "Blessed are your eyes, because they see, and your ears, because they hear ... The seed sown on rich soil is the one who hears the word and understands it, who indeed bears fruit and yields a hundred or sixty or thirtyfold."

Matthew 13: 1–23

Seeds strangled in red ink

In his book *Make Me an Instrument of Your Peace*, Kent Nerburn tells the story of his father's decision to go to college after he retired in order to realize his dream of earning a college degree.

Tentatively, guardedly, his dad enrolled in a humanities course — a subject that interested him and in which he felt he could excel. He was a model student, completing all the readings, making careful and complete notes, preparing for every class with great seriousness and attention to detail.

For his final project he chose to do a paper on the history of the English language. He worked long and hard on the paper, investing all the creativity and insight he possessed. Satisfied with the final draft, he confidently passed it in to the professor. The desire to learn and pursue his degree, dreams put aside for some forty years, were about to be realized.

But when he received back the paper, it was covered with red-inked corrections and caustic comments. The paper was graded by a graduate teaching assistant who had taken it upon himself to savage the poor man's first efforts at academic style and expression.

He showed the paper to his son, then a doctoral candidate. Kent reviewed the paper with his father, pointing out the many good parts of the paper and taking the sting out of the graduate assistant's cutting margin notes. He also showed his father the parts of the paper that needed clarity.

But it didn't matter.

Kent Nerburn's father never took another course again.

His single abiding passion in life was education, his greatest unfinished accomplishment in life was his undergraduate degree — but because of an imperious graduate assistant with a bad attitude and a red pen, his dream of a college degree would remain just a dream.[6]

In all probability, the graduate assistant never realized how devastating his comments were. He is the antithesis of the sower of today's Gospel; the discouragement and derision he sows by his arrogance squanders the opportunity to plant the harvest God calls us to reap.

Chapter 13 of Matthew's Gospel is the evangelist's collection of Jesus' parables. The word *parable* comes from the Greek word *parabole*, which means putting two things side by side in order to confront or compare them. And that is exactly how Jesus uses parables: He places a simile from life or nature against the abstract idea of the reign of God. The comparison challenges listeners/readers to consider ideas and possibilities greater and larger than those to which they might be accustomed.

Today's Gospel is the parable of the sower, a parable that appears in all three synoptic Gospels. In Palestine, sowing was done before the plowing. Seed was not precisely placed in the ground. The farmer scattered the seed in all directions, knowing that, even though much will be wasted, enough will be sown in good earth to ensure a harvest nonetheless (a "ten-fold" harvest was considered a good crop; a harvest of a hundred or sixty or thirty-fold was unimaginable).

This is one of only two parables, however, that Jesus explains in detail (the other: the parable of the weeds and the wheat, Matthew 13: 36–43). In this allegory, we are both the sowers of the seed and the "soil" in which the seed is planted. By our attitudes, our beliefs, our actions, we sow seeds of encouragement, joy and reconciliation — but some of the seeds we sow (like that of the sower of the

Gospel who does not realize where his seed is falling, like the arrogant graduate student who destroys the retiree's confidence) contribute to cycles of discouragement, anger, violence, abuse, enslavement and injustice.

But to be faithful "sowers" of the Gospel, we must also become "rich soil" ourselves, in which the seed of God's Word takes roots and becomes a harvest far greater and lasting than our own interests and profit, a harvest that benefits others far more than benefits us.

*I*n your spirit of compassion and peace, O God,
open the hard soil of our hearts and minds
and plant and nurture your Word
of compassion and justice in us.
Then make us faithful sowers of the Word
that has taken root within us:
help us to sow hope in the hard ground of despair;
justice on the ground where the birds devour such seed
thoughtlessly and selfishly;
understanding and patience in the rootless;
peace among the choking thorns.

Sunday 16 / Proper 11

The parables of the wheat and weeds, the mustard seed, and the yeast.

Matthew 13: 24–43
[Roman lectionary]

Matthew 13: 24–30, 36–43
[Common lectionary]

Parables of the kingdom: 1

*T*he people of Jesus' time longed for a return to Israel's former glory. For hundreds of years, Jews waited for the promise of the prophets to be fulfilled: that the Messiah, the "anointed" one of God, would one day restore their nation to power, re-establishing the throne of David.

And now comes this Jesus, preaching the coming of the "kingdom of heaven" to a people chafing under generations of Roman occupation. But the "kingdom" Jesus comes to establish is not the political entity the Jews of his time were hoping for. The word "kingdom" that Jesus proclaims in Matthew's Gospel is a "rule," not a territory. While his synoptic counterparts write of the "kingdom of God" as a future eschatological event, Matthew's "kingdom of heaven" begins here and now with the dawning of Emmanuel, "God with us" in the person of Jesus of Nazareth. The kingdom of heaven embraces souls, not land possessions; God's rule transcends the boundaries of time and space; the power and authority of God's reign is centered not in domination or exploitation but in compassion and forgiveness.

Matthew's Gospel has been called the "Gospel of the Kingdom," containing some 51 references to the kingdom or reign of God. Three of Jesus' parables envisioning this "kingdom" make up today's Gospel:

The parable of the wheat and the weeds:

God's kingdom will be "harvested" from among the good who exist side-by-side with the bad. Palestinian farmers were plagued by *tares* — weeds that were very difficult to distinguish from good grain. The two would often grow together and become so intertwined that it was impossible to separate them without ripping both weed and plant from the ground. Jesus teaches his impatient followers that the Lord of the harvest is more concerned with the growth of the wheat than with the elimination of the weeds. The time for separation and burning will come in God's own time; our concern should be that of our own faithfulness.

We often approach religion as deadly serious business; we lose the spirit of joy and the sense of hope that are part of the promise of the Risen Christ. We become so concerned about pulling out the weeds that we forget to harvest the grain; we become so focused on the evil and abuses that surround us and "threaten" us that we fail to realize and celebrate the healing and life-giving presence of God in our very midst; we become so intent in upbraiding and punishing sinners that our own lives become mired in gloom and despair. The task of judging sinners belongs to God; God entrusts to us the work of compassion and reconciliation.

The parable of the wheat and the weeds (a parable found only in Matthew) assures us that, in God's own good time, good will triumph over evil, that the justice and forgiveness we struggle to cultivate among "weeds" of selfishness and hatred will come to harvest, that our persistence to live in peace with those with whom we are in conflict will be vindicated.

The parable of the mustard seed:

The smallest and humblest are enabled by the Spirit to do great things in the kingdom of God. From small and humble beginnings, God's kingdom will grow.

All of us, at some time, are called to be "mustard seeds," to do the small, thankless things that are necessary to bring a sense of wholeness and fulfillment to our homes and communities. From

such "mustard seeds" yields a great harvest of peace and reconciliation.

Faith is the ability to see the potential in the smallest of
things and the courage and perseverance to unlock that potential.
Humanity's dreams of peace, community and justice will be
realized, first, in the everyday acts of such goodness of each
one of us. Such is "mustard seed" faith: that the smallest and
humblest acts of justice, kindness and compassion are undertaken
in the certainty that they will contribute to the building of God's
kingdom.

The parable of the yeast:

A small amount of yeast mixed with three measures of flour
(about fifty pounds) can make enough bread to feed over a hundred. In the same way, God's reign is a powerful albeit unseen
force.

Often, we don't realize the power that our simple word of
encouragement or an unseen act of kindness can have in the life
of another. But that is exactly what Christ calls us to do in today's
Gospel: to use whatever good we are and are able to do to be
"yeast" in the lives of others, giving life when all seems dead
and pointless, restoring hope when overwhelmed by despair and
sorrow.

Matthew's Gospel was written some fifty years after Jesus'
death and fifteen years after the destruction of Jerusalem. By this
time it is clear to the community of Christians that Jesus is not
going to be accepted by all of Israel as the Messiah. In citing
these parables, the writer of Matthew encouraged the largely
Jewish Christian community to see itself as the legitimate heir to
God's promises to Israel. They were the "good wheat" existing
side by side with the "weeds" that would destroy it; the small
mustard seed that would give rise to the great and mighty tree of
the Church, the new Israel; the small measure of yeast that would
become bread for the world.

*M*ay we always dare to hope, O God of compassion,
that the smallest, most hidden
    and least significant seed we plant will,
in your own good time,
lead to a harvest of peace and goodness in our garden.
In whatever way you lead us,
with whatever abilities you give us,
may we be that measure of yeast
that provides the leaven of your justice to our world.

[In the Gospel assigned for today in the Common lectionary, the parables
of the mustard seed and the yeast — Matthew 13: 31–33 are omitted;
the pericope continues with Jesus' explanation of the parable of the seed and
weeds, Matthew 13: 36–43. The parables of the mustard and the yeast are
included in next Sunday's Gospel reading, Proper 12.]

The parables of the buried treasure, the merchant and the pearls, and the fishing net.

Matthew 13: 44–52
[Roman lectionary]

Matthew 13: 31–33, 44–52
[Common lectionary]

Parables of the kingdom: 2

*T*hree more short parables from chapter 13 of Matthew's Gospel make up today's pericope. The first two parables — the parables of the buried treasure and the pearl — are lessons in the total *attachment* to Christ and *detachment* from the things of the world demanded of the disciple in order to make the reign of God a reality; the parable of the fishing net calls disciples to seek the things of God amid the clutter of life.

The parables of the buried treasure and the pearls:

The "treasures" and "pearls" of God are not found in the things of the earth but in the values of heaven: love, justice, mercy, peace. True wisdom begins with tirelessly seeking such treasures of lasting value that are the things of God: the love of family and friends, the support given and received in being part of a community, the sense of joy and fulfillment found in serving and giving for the sake of others. To find God means to live our lives with a vision of faith and a perseverance of spirit to realize God's presence in every moment God gives us.

In order to attain such treasure, we must take the risk of the speculator and "sell off" our own interests, ambitions and agendas in order to free us to "purchase" the lasting values of the compassion, love and reconciliation of God. Our "investment" in the things of God, Jesus promises, will return to us a deep sense of joy and meaning in our lives.

The parable of the fishing net:

The parable of the dragnet is similar in theme to last week's parable of the wheat and weeds. Again, Matthew makes the point that the kingdom of God is neither a distant, transcendent event, but a dynamic movement toward completion and fulfillment that Jesus has set into motion. In the parable of the dragnet, Jesus calls us to embrace the vision of God that seeks out the good and nurturing, the right and just in all things amid the "junk" of life.

*L*ead our hearts, guide our spirits and focus our vision
to seek you and your treasures
of your forgiveness, mercy and peace
in all things, O God.
Make our works of justice and peace
be stones in the foundation of your reign
in our time and place.
Let our efforts at reconciliation and compassion
create a highway for all to journey
to your dwelling place.

Sunday 18 / Proper 13

When it was evening, the disciples approached Jesus and said, "This is a deserted place and it is already late; dismiss the crowds so that they can go to the villages and buy food for themselves." Jesus said, "There is no need for them to go away; give them some food yourself." Taking the five loaves and two fish, and looking up to heaven, Jesus said the blessing, broke the loaves, and gave them to the disciples, who in turn gave them to the crowds.

Matthew 14: 13–21

Group dynamics

*I*t happens in every parish:

The pastor has a new project in mind — a religious education experience for teenagers, a Thanksgiving dinner for the poor, a food and clothing collection for the local shelter. The pastor then begins recruiting parishioners to make it happen. It can be a tough sell for the pastor: People are very protective of their time. They're not sure that this is something they want to do or are comfortable becoming involved with. They doubt they have the abilities and patience necessary for this kind of work. But, eventually, a group of volunteers — however reluctant — comes together.

And then, without fail, the remarkable happens. The once hesitant recruits discover that, *Hey, we can do this!* They can make this work. They can see the importance of what they are doing. Their reluctance gives way to fresh optimism and enthusiasm; their doubts disappear in a new spirit of "anything is possible." Even though they may hold back initially, they are ready to devote whatever time and skills and money are necessary to see the project through. The volunteers are transformed by the joy of doing good.

They have become a community.

They are church.

What happens in today's Gospel is such an experience of church. Jesus transforms a gathering of many different people who become one in their need, one in the bread they share, one in the love of Christ who has brought them together. Because someone was willing to share the little that he or she had, Jesus was able to make a miracle happen.

The multiplication of the loaves and fish is the only one of Jesus' miracles recorded in all four Gospels. The early Christian community especially cherished this story because they saw this event as anticipating the Eucharist and the final banquet in the kingdom of God. This miracle is also rooted in the First Testament: For the people of Israel, the metaphor of a great banquet was a cherished visualization of the promised victory of the Messiah. The gifts of the land were unmistakable signs of their God's great providence, recalling the Lord's providing manna in the desert to their wandering ancestors. Throughout the psalms and writings of the prophets, the Messiah's coming was often portrayed as a great banquet with choice food and wines. Today's miracle of the loaves and fish mirrors this ancient image for the people of the new Israel.

In Matthew's account, Jesus acts out of his great compassion for the crowds. Just as the merciful God feeds the Israelites of the Exodus with the desert manna, Jesus, "his heart moved with pity," feeds the crowds who have come to hear him. First, however, he challenges the disciples to give what they have — five loaves and two fish; then he performs the four-fold action that prefigures the Eucharist: Jesus *takes, blesses, breaks* and *gives* the bread and fish to the assembled multitude, making of them a community of the Lord's banquet.

For the Church, the sacrament of the Eucharist is both noun and verb: The Eucharist unites us as Church, the faithful community of the Risen One; in turn, we are to become the Eucharist we have received in our generosity, compassion and work for reconciliation and justice. We can perform wonders in our own time and place, we *become* Church, by imitating those four decisive verbs of Jesus:

take, bless, break, give — taking from what we have, blessing it by offering it to others in God's spirit of love, breaking it from our own needs and interests for the sake of others, and giving it with joy-filled gratitude to the God who has blessed us with so much.

*L*ord Jesus,
you give us your life and love
in the bread and wine of the Eucharist.
May we become what we receive at your table:
make us a sacrament of your compassion and peace
for our hurting and broken world.

Sunday 19 / Proper 14

After he fed the people, Jesus dismissed the crowds [and] went up on the mountain to pray. The disciples see Jesus walking on the sea during the storm:
"Take heart, it is I; do not be afraid." Jesus stretched out his hand and caught Peter, and said to him, "O you of little faith, why did you doubt?"

Matthew 14: 22–33

Catching Melinda

*T*he day had come. Melinda, all of four and a half, faced the biggest challenge of her young life: Today, the training wheels were coming off her bicycle.

After detaching the wobbly little wheels from the back tire, Dad helped Melinda on to the bicycle and held it — and her — steady. He showed her how to sit up straight and balance herself on the seat. As she began to peddle, Dad ran alongside, holding on to the back of the seat. At one point, he let go and Melinda was on her own — for all of five seconds. Almost immediately she started to lose her balance and fall. "Daddy!" she screamed. Daddy was right there and caught her.

Dad got her set again and, after some encouraging Dad-like words, the unconvinced Melinda was off again. She was doing fine until her foot slipped off the pedal. But Dad was right there again, catching her and the bike.

A third time, with new determination, Melinda got on the bike. Dad ran alongside and when she was going at a steady clip, he let go … and Melinda was on her way. And Dad cheered his daughter on as she happily circled the street on her two-wheeler. Victory!

It would not be the last time in Melinda's life that Dad would "catch" her. Dad would be ready for the next time and the time after that and time after that to "catch" his beloved Melinda whenever she fell.

From new bicycles to new schools, to broken relationships to the journey of marriage, growing up can be a terrifying experience. But as Melinda's dad was there for her, Jesus promises that, in every storm we face, his hand is extended to us in the hand of those we love and trust. Despite the storms that batter our boats as we make our way across the stormy sea, Christ promises to be that calming presence, that steadying hand, if we keep faith in Christ, who is both our guiding star and our destination.

In Matthew's Gospel, Jesus' walking on the water and his catching Peter immediately follow the multiplication of the loaves and fishes. The depth of Peter's love for Jesus is not matched by a corresponding depth of faith; but Jesus, nonetheless, raises the sinking disciple up from the waters of fear and death. Just as he was there to grab the sinking Peter, Jesus is there to "catch" us if we have the trust and faith to seek his hand and reach for it. His is the voice of assurance in the midst of confusion and despair; he is the path through life's most difficult terrain; he is the hand reaching out to grab us when we stumble and fall. Faith is to listen attentively for that voice amid the many demanding voices screaming at us; to seek out his path in the course of far too many choices and approaches prodding and pushing us; to reach for his hand convinced that he is there and will not let us fall. Jesus speaks in the reassuring and wise voices of parents, teachers and close friends; he catches us in the hands of those who run beside as we struggle to keep our balance on our bicycles. And often we are that voice; we are the helping hand of Jesus for others.

One other detail about today's Gospel: Matthew includes the note that, after feeding the crowds, Jesus sought out a quiet place to pray. Throughout the Gospels, Jesus intentionally withdraws from his friends and followers to be alone; but such times are not for "chilling" or "vegging" but for attentive, focused prayer: to be in touch with the rhythm and movement of God. God calls us to our own out-of-the-way places, our own quiet "mountains" to be fully aware of God's presence in our lives and hearts.

*D*uring the darkest nights of our lives, O Lord,
be the light that guides us to safety.
As we stumble and fall along our journey to you,
be our equilibrium that balances and steadies us
as we negotiate our way.
When we are overwhelmed by fear and doubt,
be the hand that pulls us to safety.

Jesus cures the daughter of the Canaanite woman: "Lord, even the dogs eat the crumbs from the tables of their masters."

Matthew 15: 21–28

It's not easy on the outside ...

*J*oe had done his time. After ten years, he was released from prison and stepped out into the real world, the free world. His cellmate and buddies on the inside envied Joe, of course, but were happy for him and wished him well as he went home.

But before long, Joe was back behind bars, not for another crime but for a technical violation of his release — he flunked a drug test. When he saw Joe again, his old cellmate "gritted" at him — in prison-speak, a sign of disapproval and disappointment. *How could Joe mess up the chance to get out of this place?!* To guys still on the inside, to come back to prison was the worst failure imaginable. When Joe tried to explain what had happened, his friend uttered a noncommittal "gritt."

That's when Joe's face crumpled in despair.

"I was just so damn lonely out there," he said with a sigh. "I had a good job, I was doing fine. But there was no one to talk to. Dude, all I know is prison; I didn't know what to say to those people out there. So I started hanging out with the old crowd. At least they could understand where I was coming from. And then one thing led to another ... "

The cellmate gritted. Yeh, he understood.[7]

And so would the woman from Canaan in today's Gospel.

We do indeed have high standards — for other people. We are quick to assess people purely by our own measure of what is right and good; we determine their worth by their function or their usefulness in helping us accomplish our own goals and agendas; we instinctively size up people by our own inaccurate and sometimes bigoted stereotypes; we become so obsessed with numbers and demographics that we forget that we are dealing with flesh-and-blood human beings with hopes and beliefs. But the call to discipleship demands that we look beyond labels and stereotypes to realize that every one of us is a child of God, brothers and sisters all.

The woman who approaches Jesus in today's Gospel was despised by the Jewish community because of her race. She was not only a Gentile but a descendent of the Canaanites, one of Israel's oldest and most despised enemies. As a Canaanite, the woman was viewed as a "dog" by the "righteous"; in her "inferiority," many Jews mistakenly felt a sense of "superiority" in the eyes of God. Despite Jesus' uncharacteristic rebuff of her (the Jews of Jesus' time equated anyone who was not a Jew as a "dog"), the woman has the presence of mind to point out that "even dogs are given crumbs and scraps from their masters' tables." She displays both great faith in Jesus (addressing him by the Messianic title of "Son of David") and great love for her daughter (subjecting herself to ridicule and recrimination for approaching Jesus) that should inspire both Jew and Gentile — and Christian.

(This story was very important to the members of Matthew's predominately Gentile Christian community, who saw Jesus' healing of the daughter of the Canaanite mother as a prophetic model for the relationship between Jewish and Gentile Christians.)

In her great compassion and love for her sick daughter and her willingness to face ridicule and harassment for approaching Jesus, she is, first, a loving mother; in her courage to come forward in the face of imminent rejection and denunciation, she is a model of great faith. Jesus' compassion for her and his healing of her daughter break down the wall between Gentile and Jew; the prophet Isaiah's vision (today's first reading) of a single human family, bound by what is right and just, begins to be realized.

Christ calls us to make places in our society, in our communities, in our hearts for the Joes and the Canaanite women in our midst: those souls struggling to make something of their lives, who are trying to put the pieces of their broken selves back together despite the ostracism, rejection and ridicule they encounter.

God our Father,
Open our spirits and hearts
to see every man, woman and child
as you see them:
as your beloved children,
made in your image,
and our brothers and sisters in your spirit.

Jesus said to his disciples, "Who do you say I am?" Simon Peter answered, "You are the Christ, the Son of the living God." And Jesus answered him, "Blessed are you, Simon son of Jonah. For flesh and blood has not revealed this to you, but my Father in heaven. And so I say to you, you are Peter, and upon this rock I will build my church … "

Matthew 16: 13–20

Knowing …

*E*very day, for years, he visited his wife in the nursing home. She suffered from Alzheimer's disease; with each day she slipped further and further away in the fog of dementia. Every day he would help her with her lunch. He would sit with her and show her the pictures of their children, telling her the latest family news and stories she would forget as soon as she heard them. He would patiently remind her who he was and explain that they were married and had been for the past 52 years and they had two daughters and a son and four beautiful grandchildren. He would hold her hand as she drifted in and out of consciousness. Before leaving, he would kiss her and tell her how much he loved her — and she would never realize nor remember later that he had even been there.

His heartbroken friends would ask him, *Why do you keep going when she doesn't even know who you are?*

And he would always reply, "Because I know who *I* am."[8]

This husband's faithfulness is the perfect and complete answer to the question Jesus poses to Peter and the others — and to us — in today's Gospel.

In Matthew's Gospel, Peter's confession of faith is a turning point in the ministry of Jesus. Jesus will now concentrate on preparing his disciples to take on the teaching ministry and leadership of the Church he will establish. The scene of today's Gospel, Caesarea Philippi, was the site of temples dedicated to no less than 14 different pagan gods, ranging from the Syrian god Baal to Pan, the Greek god of nature. In the middle of the city was a great white temple built by Herod and dedicated to the "divinity" of Caesar (hence the name of the city). In the midst of this marketplace of gods and temples, Jesus first indicates his plans and hopes for his church.

As often happens in the Gospel, Peter serves as Jesus' foil. Jesus "sets up" Peter's declaration of faith by asking his disciples what people are saying about him. Many believed that Jesus is the reincarnation of John the Baptizer or the long-awaited return of the prophets Elijah or Jeremiah (Malachi 4: 5–6), whose return would signal the restoration of Israel. Simon Peter, however, has been given the gift of faith ("flesh and blood has not revealed this to you") and unequivocally states that Jesus is the Messiah. He is the first of the disciples to grasp the divinity of Christ. On the faith of Peter "the rock" Christ establishes his Church.

Jesus blesses Simon with the new name of "rock" (*Kepha* in Aramaic, *Petros* in Greek), indicating that his faith will be the foundation for Jesus' new Church. Peter is entrusted with the keys of the kingdom of heaven (an image drawn from Isaiah 22: 15–25, today's first reading in the Roman lectionary) and the mission to bring sins to consciousness and to proclaim to sinners the love and forgiveness of God.

In realizing exactly who Jesus is and the meaning of the Gospel he embodies, we start to understand who we are and what our lives are about. Today's Gospel asks us exactly what we mean when we say that "we believe in Jesus Christ, [God's] only Son and our Lord," what we mean when we claim that we have been baptized into his death and resurrection. The question Jesus poses to Peter and his disciples is asked of us every minute of every day. Every decision we make is ultimately a response to the question, *Who do you say I am?* Our love for family and friends, our dedication to the cause of justice, our commitment to the highest moral and ethical standards, our taking the first step toward reconciliation and forgiveness, our simplest acts of kindness and charity declare most accurately and effectively our belief in the Gospel Jesus as the Messiah and Redeemer.

*R*isen Christ,
give us the simple but profound faith
   of Peter the fisherman.
May we possess his resolve to be worthy of your call
   to be your disciples;
may we share his determination to build your church
   here in our time and place;
may we embrace his perseverance to proclaim
   your presence
in every moment you give us,
in every decision that confronts us,
in every relationship with which we are blessed.

Sunday 22 / Proper 17

Jesus turned and said to Peter, "Get behind me, Satan! You are an obstacle to me. You are thinking not as God does, but has human beings do … Whoever wishes to come after me must deny himself, take up his cross, and follow me."

Matthew 16: 21–27

Gilead

*M*arilynne Robinson's Pulitzer Prize-winning novel *Gilead* is written in the form of a long letter by a Congregationalist pastor in his mid-70s to his seven-year-old son. Aware that he is dying, John Ames wants to tell his son things that he never had an opportunity to tell him or that his son will only be able to appreciate when he is older. In a sense, Pastor Ames' letter is his last will and testament.

In the course of his letter, Ames calculates that if all the sermons he preached were bound in books, they would total 225 volumes, "which puts me up there with Augustine and Calvin for quantity."

But he is convinced that his best sermon is one he never delivered.

He wrote it during World War I — the "Great War" — when many people in Iowa were dying of influenza. The young men who succumbed to the disease, he wrote, were actually being spared a far worse fate. The Lord "was gathering them in before they could go off and commit murder against their brothers," he had written.

Many years later, this sermon is still "bold and bright" in Ames' memory, and he still believes in its message. He could not bring himself to deliver it, however, because he knew that the only people who would hear it were the beleaguered folk, mostly old women, who were already "sad and apprehensive as they could stand to be and no more approving of the war than I was."[9]

Ames put the sermon aside, all too aware that it would never be heard in the noise of the conflict.

It is a natural and understandable reaction to avoid whatever is unpleasant, uncomfortable, or stressful. In today's Gospel, Peter simply wants to protect Jesus from the suffering he has predicted — but Jesus sharply rebukes Peter for trying to diminish or skirt the cross.

Peter's confession of faith (last Sunday's Gospel) begins a new phase of Matthew's Gospel. As he makes his way to Jerusalem, Jesus' teachings will now be addressed primarily to his disciples to prepare them for what awaits them in Jerusalem — and beyond.

The hostility between Jesus and the leaders of Judaism is approaching a flash point. In today's Gospel, Jesus makes clear that his mission as the Messiah includes suffering and death. Jesus sees Peter's refusal to accept such a possibility as a "satanic" attempt to deflect the Messiah from his mission of redemption — Peter the "rock" stumbles over the "stumbling block" of the Crucified One (Matthew 11: 6). To avoid suffering and hardship in order to opt for the easy and safe course is purely human thinking, an obstacle to experiencing the life of the Spirit. Authentic discipleship involves taking on the cross and "denying oneself" — disowning ourselves as the center of our existence and realizing that God is the object and purpose of our lives.

Faith is not the warm, comforting quilt we would like it to be; faith often demands that we listen to the "sermons" we find hard to understand and to "preach" a Gospel that runs counter to the dictates of our practical, pragmatic world. Jesus calls us to embrace the faith of the cross, faith that understands that the crosses of our lives can be the vehicles for bringing God's promise of resurrection into our lives and the lives of those we love.

In "denying" ourselves we discover the life and love of God.

God of graciousness and compassion,
may we not hesitate to take up the crosses
laid upon our shoulders.
By your gift of faith,

may we know that you bear our crosses with us;
By your grace,
may we make our crosses vehicles of resurrection.
May we struggle, in our own time and place,
to build your kingdom of peace and justice,
regardless of the cost we have to pay
and the crosses we have to bear —
but knowing that you will transform
those crosses and costs
into light and justice.

Sunday 23 / Proper 18

> "Whatever you bind on earth shall be bound in heaven, and whatever you loose on earth shall be loosed in heaven ... Where two or three are gathered together in my name, there I am in the midst of them."

Matthew 18: 15–20

The deafening silence

*T*he silence can be deafening.

Family members and friends live their lives tiptoeing around one another. Spouses, parents, children are held hostage by the silence.

Not in our family, they all insist.

Better to suffer in silence, they hope.

It may be alcoholism, drug addiction, physical abuse that victimizes the family; or a misunderstanding over a broken relationship, a divorce, a child's rejection of the family's culture or religion that creates a tension that rules a family's life.

Regardless of the cause, fear is the controlling agent.

Say nothing.

Don't bring it up.

He'll explode if you even mention it.

It'll only get ugly.

You'll never change their minds.

What good will it do — you'll only get hurt.

And so there is silence.

Silence — while hearts scream in agony and spirits shrivel and die.

In today's Gospel, Jesus urges his followers not to tolerate the silence that destroys community, the silence that precludes healing and reconciliation. He pleads with us not to allow our judgments and disappointments to isolate us from others but to confront those problems, misunderstandings and issues that divide us, grieve us and embitter us.

It is hard, hard work to take on such silence.

Chapter 18 of Matthew's Gospel is a collection of Jesus' sayings on the practical challenges facing the Christian community, including status-seeking, scandal, division and, the topic of today's reading, conflict. Today's reading outlines a process of reconciliation among divided members of a community. The verses read more like regulations devised by an ecclesiastical committee than a discourse by Jesus (this chapter has been called the "church-order discourse" of Jesus). But the point of Jesus' exhortation is that we must never tolerate any breech of personal relationship between us and another member of the Christian community. At each stage of the process — one-on-one confrontation, seeking resolution in the presence of impartial confreres who can then serve as witnesses to all the facts, bringing the issue before the whole community (the "church" — one of only two uses of the word *ekklesia* in Matthew's Gospel) — the goal is to win the erring Christian back to the community (the three-step process of reconciliation outlined by Jesus here corresponds to the procedure of the Qumran community).

Jesus calls his hearers to seek honesty and sincerity in all relationships, to put aside self-interest, anger and wounded pride, and take the first step in healing the rifts that destroy the sense of love that binds family and friends, church and community — the love of Christ is the "debt" that binds us to one another. The "process" Jesus lays out for bringing sinners back to the community seeks to build communities that are *inclusive,* not exclusive: to bring the lost back, not out of pride or zealousness, but out of "the debt that binds us to love one another." Jesus' exhortation closes with a promise of God's presence in the midst of every community, regardless of size, bound together by faith.

Christ asks us to take on the hard, hard work of reconciliation, to be committed to seeking solutions to our problems not out of any sense of indignation or self-righteousness but out of a commitment to imitate and bring into our lives the great love and mercy of God.

*G*od of mercy and compassion,
make us your prophets of reconciliation
and vehicles of forgiveness.
May we speak your Word of compassion
in the devastating silence of anger;
may we offer the balm of understanding and acceptance
to the wounded, marginalized and hurt;
may we restore the bond of your love to communities
broken by misunderstanding, intolerance
　　and self-centeredness.

The parable of the unforgiving debtor: " 'Should you not have had pity on your fellow servant, as I had pity on you?' "So will my heavenly Father do to you, unless each of you forgives one another from your heart."

Matthew 18: 21–35

Breaking the spell

*R*abbi Naomi Levy recounts this story in her book *To Begin Again: The Journey Toward Comfort, Strength and Faith in Difficult Times:*[10]

A mother brought her six-year-old son, Joey, into Rabbi Naomi's office. Joey was pale and shaking. The rabbi greeted the boy with a hug and invited him to tell her what the matter was. Joey said that his friend Andy had died in a car accident. That began a long conversation between Joey and Rabbi Naomi about death, but the rabbi got the feeling that Joey had something very specific to get off his chest.

Finally, Joey said, "When we were playing together last week, I kicked Andy on purpose."

"And you feel bad about that now?" the rabbi asked.

Joey started to cry and said yes.

What would Joey say to Andy if he were still alive?

"I'd say, 'I'm sorry I kicked you.' "

And the minute Joey said those words, Rabbi Naomi writes "it was as if a spell had been broken. This little boy felt relieved. He couldn't apologize to Andy in person, but he could verbalize his regret and that seemed to lighten his load quite a bit."

There is a healing we can only experience through forgiveness. As Joey discovers at a very young age, life is too fleeting and precious to waste away in needless recriminations, pointless anger and stifling guilt.

Forgiveness is hard work: it means overcoming our own anger and outrage at the injustice waged against us and focusing our concern, instead, on the person who wronged us and ruptured our relationship with him/her; it means possessing the humility to face the hurt we have inflicted on others as a result of our insensitivity and self-centeredness. But only in forgiving and seeking forgiveness do we experience liberation and the possibility of bringing healing and new life to a pained and grieving situation.

The cutting edge of Jesus' teaching on love is that nothing is unforgivable nor should there be limits to extending forgiveness. It is ironic that Peter should ask the question about forgiveness that introduces the parable of the merciless steward, since Peter himself will be so generously forgiven by Jesus for his Good Friday denial. The common rabbinical teaching of the time was that one must forgive another three times; the fourth time, the offender was not to be forgiven. Perhaps Peter was anticipating Jesus' response to his question by suggesting seven rather than the conventional three times — but Jesus counters that there should be no limit to the number of times we must be ready to forgive those who wrong us ("seventy times seven times"), just as there is no limit to the Father's forgiveness of us.

To forgive as God forgives means to act intentionally to purge the animosity that exists between us and those who hurt us, to take the first, second and last steps toward bridging divisions, to work ceaselessly to mend broken relationships, to welcome back the forgiven into our lives unconditionally, totally and joyfully. As the king in the parable withdraws his forgiveness of his servant because of the servant's failure to forgive another, God's forgiveness must be shared if it is to be realized in our own relationship with God. Forgiveness can only be given out of love and, therefore, demands sacrifice on the part of the forgiver.

Before God, every one of us is an insolvent debtor — but the great mystery of our faith is that God continues to love us, continues to call us back to him, continues to seek not retribution but reconciliation with us. All God asks of us is that we forgive one another as he forgives us, to help one another back up when we stumble just as God lifts us back up.

*W*ith humility before your never-failing compassion,
with gratitude for your constant providence,
may we become your people of reconciliation, O God.
Help us to forgive joyfully and unconditionally;
help us to seek forgiveness readily and humbly.
By your grace,
may we break the spell of anger and sadness
through our smallest and simplest efforts
    at reconciliation:
to welcome back the lost and separated,
to restore our families and communities to completeness;
to heal relationships we have broken
by our insensitivity and self-centeredness.

Sunday 25 / Proper 20

The parable of the generous vineyard owner: "Are you envious because I am generous? Thus the last will be first, and the first will be last."

Matthew 20: 1–16

Where's mine?

*T*he company devises a new program of "flex time" for employees with young children or institutes a tuition-reimbursement program for employees working on advanced degrees. It's a great benefit to those who qualify — but other employees begin to grumble, *What about us? What's management going to do for us? Why should they get special treatment? Where's ours?*

A student is having a hard time with math. The teacher spends many after-school hours working with the student until the light finally comes on. The student does well on the next test. But the other students resent him. They say he is just trying to play to the teacher's sympathy. They deride him as *teacher's pet* and worse — names that can't be repeated here.

He has treated his family dreadfully — abusing their generosity, their patience and their trust. And yet, he is taken back again and again. After still another reconciliation with his wife and children and parents, the other members of the family and close friends can hardly stand to be in the same room with him.

We read about an individual's work on behalf of a disadvantaged group in our society or a company's donation to a nonprofit group working for the poor or the sick or the environment or the arts. And we immediately start to wonder: *What's the angle? What's the REAL agenda here? What are they getting out of it? There are worthier programs and bigger needs out there than that — what are they doing for them? Why are they so special?*

We struggle to meet our obligations, and yet there is help available for others that we don't qualify for because we're too well off. A co-worker gets a promotion that could well have been ours, and we resent them. A friend comes into a windfall, and we wonder why we haven't done as well. Many of us have an immediate reaction to government welfare and "bailout" programs: *Why should our hard-earned tax money go to help those people? We've run our businesses responsibly and fairly — why should they be rewarded for their greed and incompetence? I work hard for my money — why can't they?*

All understandable reactions.

But Christ calls us to embrace the vision of the generous vineyard owner: to rejoice in the good fortune of others and their being enabled to realize their dreams for themselves and their families. Frankly, God's sense of generosity, love and forgiveness strikes us as an extravagance that offends our own sense of fairness. But trusting in the goodness of God frees us from what our time clocks, scales, yardsticks and spreadsheets dictate what is "fair," enabling us to realize all that we have received and how much God has blessed us, and compelling us to experience the joy of sharing our treasure with those who have not realized such blessings in their lives.

The workers in today's Gospel are so obsessed with what another has been given that they fail to realize all that they have received from God. The parable of the generous vineyard owner (which appears only in Matthew's Gospel) is the first of several parables and exhortations challenging the Pharisees and scribes and those who criticized Jesus for preaching to tax collectors and sinners.

Jesus makes two points in this parable:

First, the parable speaks of the primacy of mercy in the kingdom of God. The employer (God) responds to those who have worked all day that he has been just in paying them the agreed-upon wage; they have no grievance if he chooses to be generous to others. God's compassion and mercy transcends the narrow and limited laws and logic of human justice; it is not the amount of service given but the attitude of love and generosity behind that service.

The parable also illustrates the universality of the new Church. The contracted workers, Israel, will be joined by the new "migrant workers," the Gentiles, who will share equally in the joy of the kingdom of God.

Christ invites us, his Church, to become what St. Paul calls "a people of thanksgiving," to live our lives not in desperation or cynicism but in wonder and gratitude to such a God who breathes life into our being for no other reason than his unfathomable love.

*G*od of all good things,
transform our hearts into vessels of gratitude,
that we may find joy in your blessings to everyone.
Do not let jealousy or envy, anger or resentment,
be a wedge between us and others,
but let their success and happiness help us to realize
your countless blessings to us, as well.

The parable of the two sons: "Tax collectors and prostitutes are entering the kingdom of God before you. When John came to you in the way of righteousness, you did not believe him; but the tax collectors and the prostitutes did."

Matthew 21: 28–32
[Roman lectionary]

Matthew 21: 23–32
[Common lectionary]

Theories and assumptions run amok

*A*n engineer, a chemist, and an economist are marooned on a desert island. They manage to secure from their sinking craft a case of canned food but no opener.

The engineer devises a plan: "I climb up to a precise height, throw a can at an exact angle onto a pre-selected rock. The can should split open."

"No," the chemist says. "I'll place a can in direct sunlight and let the trapped gases inside the can expand. In a measurable interval, the can should burst."

The economist then weighs in. "No, too messy and too much loss. With my plan we'll open the cans quickly, cleanly and without any spillage."

"Tell us what we should do," they implore.

"First," begins the economist, "let's assume we have a can opener ... "

Jesus' simple story of the two sons takes the Gospel out of the realm of the "theoretical" and places the mercy of God into the midst of our messy, complicated everyday lives. Compassion, forgiveness and mercy are only words until our actions give full expression to those values in our relationships with others; our calling ourselves Christians and disciples of Jesus means nothing until our lives express that identity in the values we uphold and the beliefs we live. Discipleship requires us to embrace the Gospel not as a set of idealistic assumptions or abstract concepts but as the rule by which we struggle to live our imperfect lives.

Today's parable of the two sons is a devastating condemnation of the Jewish religious leaders whose faith is confined to words and rituals. Jesus states unequivocally that those the self-righteous consider to be the very antithesis of religious will be welcomed by God into his presence before the "professional" religious.

Prostitutes and tax collectors were the most despised outcasts in Judaism. In light of the First Testament tradition of God's relationship with Israel as a "marriage" and Israel's disloyalty as "harlotry," prostitution was considered an especially heinous sin. Tax collectors were, in the eyes of Palestinian Jews, the very personification of corruption and theft. According to the Roman system of tax collection, publicans (tax collectors) would pay the state a fixed sum based on the theoretical amount of taxes due from a given region. The publican, in return, had the right to collect the taxes in that region — and they were not above using terrorism and extortion to collect. Tax collectors, as agents of the state, were also shunned as collaborators with Israel's Roman captors.

Jesus' declaration that those guilty of the most abhorrent of sins would enter God's kingdom before them deepened the Jewish establishment's animosity toward Jesus.

The words of the Gospel must be lived; Jesus' teachings on justice, reconciliation and love must be the light that guides us, the path we walk, the prayer we work to make a reality. Discipleship begins within our hearts, where we realize Christ's presence in our lives and in the lives of others and then honoring that presence in meaningful acts of compassion and charity.

In the Common lectionary, today's Gospel reading begins with a confrontation between Jesus and the chief priests. In Matthew's narrative, Jesus has just entered triumphantly into Jerusalem and cleared out the temple of the moneylenders and merchants. Tensions are beginning to run high. The chief priests challenge Jesus' authority to act as he does. Jesus responds by posing a question: Was John's baptism from God or was it a human invention? If the chief priests say "from God," they admit that they were wrong to discredit John; but if they dismiss John's teachings as purely human, they risk the anger of the crowds who regarded John as a prophet — and who now regard Jesus in the same light. For the faithful hearer, the voice and teaching of both Jesus and John are rooted in God. The chief priests realize that, for the moment, they have no effective strategy for dealing with this troublesome Nazarene rabbi.

*I*n you, Lord Jesus,
the Word of God becomes human for us.
May we respond to your Gospel
with more than empty words,
but with sincerity of heart and generosity of spirit.
Let your Word resonating within our hearts
compel us to "speak" with the language of compassion,
    justice and reconciliation.

Sunday 27 / Proper 22

The parable of the vineyard owner and his murderous tenants: "The kingdom of God will be taken away from you and given to a people that will produce its fruits."

Matthew 21: 33–43

The rise of hospice

*J*ust after World War II, a young English nurse was on duty at a London hospital. Entrusted to her care was a young Polish émigré dying of cancer. David, who worked as a waiter, had no family or friends in London. His only consolation was the love they discovered for each other. The nurse, a shy, tall and gawky girl named Cicely, found genuine happiness in caring for him; she discovered that her presence at his side helped him face death calmly and peacefully.

When David died, he bequeathed to Cicely all his worldly goods — five hundred pounds — with the cryptic wish that it might be "a window in your home."

What Cicely learned from caring for David began to raise questions in her mind about the way her profession cared for the dying. She could no longer accept the practice of patients and families being told "there was nothing that could be done." Even though medicine could not provide a cure, it could provide some form of comfort in the form of pain relief. The medical and health care community could also provide guidance and support to those caring for the dying as they tried to provide their loved ones some happiness and quality of life in their final days.

Cicely left nursing and went to medical school in order to study and research pain relief, receiving her medical degree at the age of 39. In her work at hospitals and clinics, she concentrated on the most effective methods of controlling pain and more compassionate and dignified ways of caring for the terminally ill.

Twenty years later, Cicely realized her life's work: the opening of St. Christopher's Hospice in south London, a residence for those dying of cancer. St. Christopher's is considered the first modern hospice — and that young nurse, Dame Cicely Saunders, is recognized as the founder of the hospice movement. Her vision led to new standards of care for the dying, matching quality medical care with emotional and spiritual support for the dying and their families. St. Christopher's has inspired the opening of similar hospices throughout the world; over 50,000 doctors, nurses and health care professionals have been trained in palliative care for the terminally ill at the facility. St. Christopher's also developed the first program in home hospice care.

Dr. Saunders said of her work:

"I once asked a man who knew he was dying what he needed above all in those who were caring for him. He said, 'For someone to look as if they are trying to understand me ... ' "

"You matter because you are you, and you matter to the last moment of your life ..."

And a promise kept: A window at the entrance of St. Christopher's Hospice honors the memory of the Polish waiter who inspired a nurse's mission.

Dame Cicely, moved by compassion and driven by her love for a poor, dying man, created a whole new environment for the dying to go to God in peace. From her corner of the vineyard, from the "patch" of the kingdom God entrusted to her, Dr. Saunders nurtured and harvested the modern hospice movement.

The vineyard is the central image of today's Gospel and first reading (Isaiah 5: 1–7). Jesus' parable of the vineyard in Matthew's Gospel "updates" Isaiah's allegory of the friend's vineyard. God is the owner of the vineyard who has "leased" the property to the religious and political leaders of Israel. Many servants (prophets) were sent to the tenants to remind them of their debt to the vineyard owner, but all met the same fate. The owner finally sends his own Son, who is brutally murdered "outside" the vineyard (a prediction of his crucifixion outside the city of Jerusalem?). With this parable, Jesus places himself in the line of the rejected prophets. God the owner finally comes himself and destroys the tenants and leaves the vineyard to others (the Church) who yield an abundant harvest. This parable is intended to give hope and encouragement to Matthew's community of first believers, who have been scorned and persecuted by its staunchly Jewish neighbors.

Every one of us has been given a portion of God's vineyard to cultivate. Fear, selfishness and arrogance can destroy whatever chances we have of turning our patch into something productive; but, through compassion, generosity and justice, we can realize a meaningful and fulfilling harvest, regardless of how small or insignificant our piece of the vineyard.

Like the tenants in today's parable, we reject whatever "stones" scare us or threaten us, whatever we don't understand, whatever challenges us and the safe lives we have built. But Christ the Messiah comes as the "cornerstone" of love rather than selfishness, of hope rather than cynicism, of peace rather than hostility, of forgiveness rather than vengeance.

O Lord of the vineyard,
you gave us this earth as a place of peace
to seek you and grow in your love.
By your grace
　　that enables us to do what we don't think we can do,
by your wisdom that shows us the way
　　through the most treacherous passes,
by your light that illuminates the darkest places,
may we transform the villages and vineyards
　　you have given us
into places where your justice abounds
　　and your peace reigns.
In the small corner of the vineyard
　　you have entrusted to us,
may we plant seeds of compassion
　　and forgiveness and comfort,
and not be afraid of our own inadequacies
　　to realize their harvest.

"The kingdom of heaven may be likened to a king who gave a wedding feast for his son: 'Behold, I have prepared my banquet, my calves and fattened cattle are killed, and everything is ready; come to the feast ... Go into the main roads and invite whomever you find ...' "When the king came to meet the guests, he saw a man there not dressed in a wedding garment. 'My friend, how is it that you came in here without a wedding garment?' But the man was reduced to silence. Then the king said to his attendants, 'Bind his hands and feet, and cast him into the darkness outside, where there will be wailing and grinding of teeth.' Many are invited, but few are chosen."

Matthew 22: 1–14

Joe's heroes

Joseph Bradley is a crane operator for a New York construction company. As a young man, he had helped build the World Trade Center. Immediately after the attacks of 9/11, he went to his union hall to volunteer. That night, he — and his crane — were assigned to work at Ground Zero.

For an oral history project on the events of those horrible days, Joe shared his experiences:

"[A] fire chief said he'd like to clear a debris field three feet deep with heavy iron on top ... four or five ironworkers asked if I had a crane and I said yes. So they said they'd like to work with me ... Like a miracle, 25 firefighters showed up right then with tanks and torches. Then we had a mission. So we went to work. No supervision. No foreman. We worked as smooth as you can imagine.

"I prayed for darkness because I couldn't handle what I was seeing. The first body was a lady in a business suit. Middle-aged. It was remarkable. She wasn't even dirty. We laid her down on the stretcher and fixed her eyes and her lapels. I remember the fire-fighter on the back of the stretcher fell, but he lifted his arms up over his head as he went down so the body wouldn't hit the ground.

"After that I was sitting on the curb with my head in my hands. It was the middle of the night. That's when the Salvation Army kids appeared in their sneakers with their pink hair and belly buttons showing and bandannas tied around their faces. One was a little girl pushing a shopping cart full of eyewash through the muck. They came with water and cold towels and took my boots off and put dry socks on my feet ... I have never seen so many people pull together. One unit, one thought.

"When I was finally relieved and started to walk out, I thought to myself, *You did pretty good. You did your part. You can go home and get back to normal ...*

"When I got to Houston Street, a bunch more of these kids, all pierced and tattooed with multicolored hair, had made a little makeshift stage. And they started to cheer as we came out, and that was it for me. I never identified with those people before, but I started crying and I cried for blocks ...

"I've been a construction worker my whole life ... I never knew anything about Episcopalians or Presbyterians, or gays, or people with nuts and bolts through their cheeks, or those Broadway people, but now I know them all. We're not the heroes. They are the heroes. They've cried and prayed out loud for me. I never thought I'd have a family like this one."[11]

The wedding feast of today's Gospel has been realized among Joe and his "heroes" at Ground Zero — everyone has a place at God's family table, regardless of race, color, creed, or hair color. If we are to be truly faithful to God's vision for the human family, then we must embrace a new, faith-centered vision that sees beyond skin color, physical abilities and mental acumen, ethnic stereotypes and economic distinctions and see all men, women and children as made in the same image and likeness of God in which we are created; we must be willing both to give joyfully of what we have and to accept humbly what everyone brings to the table.

Today's Gospel of the wedding feast is a third parable Jesus addresses to the religious leaders who have challenged his authority and seek to discredit him. The parable is another illustration of Israel's rejection of God's promise. Rejected by the people God has called to be his own, God extends the invitation to his Son's wedding feast to everyone — Gentiles, foreigners, and even those who do not know God. (Matthew's readers would immediately interpret the "destruction of those murderers" and the "burning of their city" as references to the destruction of Jerusalem by the Romans in 70 A.D.)

Jesus tells a second parable within the story of the wedding feast. The wedding garment is the conversion of heart and mind required for entry into the kingdom. The Christian who does not wear this mantle of repentance and good deeds will suffer the same fate as those who reject outright the invitation to the wedding. As the apostle Paul writes (Romans 13: 14), we must "put on" the garment of Christ.

In this Gospel Jesus articulates a radically new vision of humanity that ignores suspicions, doubts and stereotypes and, instead, recognizes every person, first, as a child of God, worthy of respect, love and compassion. God invites all his children to his table — distinctions drawn according to economic class or influence, discrimination by race or origin, reservations due to mental or physical ability disappear before God. In order to be able to take our own place at God's table, we must first realize God's vision for the human family at our own tables.

*W*ith gratitude for your generosity,
with humility at our unworthiness,
We make our way to your wedding feast,
O gracious God.
May our struggle to forgive,
our commitment to establish peace through justice,
our work to mirror the selfless spirit of service
of your Son, the Bridegroom,
become our wedding garment to wear
when we join all our brothers and sisters
at your great banquet of eternity.

"Repay to Caesar what belongs to Caesar and to God what belongs to God."

Matthew 22: 15–21

You're not being much help here, Lord …

As Jesus was teaching, someone approached Jesus with two bumper stickers, one for the Democratic candidate, one for the Republican candidate. "Teacher, we know that you are a truthful man and that you teach the way of God. Tell us, who should we vote for?" Jesus replied, "Vote for those who will lead you to God's reign. Support those who will establish the Father's kingdom of justice and mercy."

A parent then came up to Jesus and handed him two bills and asked, "Lord, money is tight. Which do I pay first: my house payment or my contribution to my church?" Jesus said, "Give thanks to God for what you have received. Pay to your debtors what is rightly owed them."

A teenager next came up to Jesus. "Jesus, my Confirmation class meets tonight, the same time as football practice for this weekend's big game. Should I come to class or do I meet my obligations to my teammates and coaches?" Jesus blessed him, saying, "Give to God the time he has given you. Give to your team the time the game warrants."

All three — the voter, the homeowner, the teenager — left Jesus as confused as they were when they approached him.

Jesus' answers are not the clear, unambiguous solutions we seek to these and many other questions. But his response is the heart of living our faith: the struggle to return to God what is God's.

In today's Gospel, two opponents of Jesus, the Pharisees and Herodians (supporters of Herod's dynasty), join forces to trap Jesus into making such a simplistic, black-and-white, either-or choice. If Jesus affirms that taxes should be paid, he alienates the religious nationalists; if he denies that taxes should be paid, then he is subject to arrest by the Romans as a political revolutionary. The very fact that his inquisitors could produce the emperor's coin from one of their purses was to admit a Roman obligation: If one used the sovereign's coin then one automatically took on an obligation to the sovereign; in other words, the Pharisees and Herodians, in trying to trap Jesus, answered their own question. But Jesus takes the debate to an even higher level by challenging them to be just as observant in paying their debt to God.

The confrontation over Caesar's coin is not a solution to any church-versus-state controversy; Jesus' response to the Pharisees today confronts them — and us — with the demand to act out of our deepest convictions and take responsibility for those actions. The purpose and meaning of life, the path to dealing with the complexities of our time and place, are found in our struggle with our consciences and in the values we hold in the depths of our hearts. Each one of us has to do for ourselves the hard work of deciding exactly what is the way of God in our complex and interconnected world of politics, money and human relationships. Jesus appeals to us to look beyond the simplistic politics and black-and-white legalisms represented by Caesar's coin and realize that we are called to embrace the values centered in a faith that sees the hand of God in all things and recognizes every human being as being part of one human family under the providence of God.

*I*n the many complexities and challenges of our lives,
O God,
may your Spirit of wisdom and compassion
be the light by which we make our way,
the measure by which weigh our choices,
the star by which we set our course.

"Teacher, which commandment in the law is the greatest?"
"You shall love the Lord, your God, with all your heart, with
all your soul, and with all your mind. This is the greatest and
the first commandment. The second is like it: You shall love
your neighbor as yourself. The whole law and the prophets
depend on these two commandments."

Matthew 22: 34—40
[Roman lectionary]

Matthew 22: 34—46
[Common lectionary]

Blood brother

*I*n her book *Bird by Bird: Some Instructions on Writing and
Life,* Anne Lamott retells "the best true story on giving I know":

An eight-year-old boy had a younger sister who was dying of
leukemia. His parents explained to him that she needed a blood
transfusion and that his blood was probably compatible. They
asked if they could test his blood. Sure, he said. The results showed
that his blood would be a good match. Then they asked the boy if
he would give his sister a pint of blood, that it could be her only
chance at living. He asked if he could think about it overnight.

The next day he went to his parents and said he was willing
to donate his blood to his sister. So they took him to the hospital
where he was put on a gurney beside his sister. Both of them were
hooked up to IVs. A nurse withdrew a pint of blood from the
boy, which was then put into his sister's IV. The boy lay on his
gurney quietly watching his blood drip into his sister. The doctor
came over to see how he was doing. The boy opened his eyes and
asked, "How soon until I start to die?"[12]

Every word of the Gospel comes down to love — love that is simple enough to articulate but so demanding that we shy away from it. The mystery of God's love is that the Being of Supreme and Omnipotent Power should love his creation so completely and so selflessly — and all God seeks in return is that such love be shared by his people throughout his creation. The brother, believing that giving his blood would mean he would die, nonetheless is willing to give his life to his sister so that she might live; in his generosity, he models the great love and compassion of the God who spares nothing to bring us to him.

In today's Gospel, as in the Gospel readings of the last few Sundays, the Jewish leaders seek to trip Jesus up. The question the lawyer poses was much discussed in rabbinical circles: Which is the greatest commandment? The Pharisees' intention in posing the question was to force Jesus into a single rabbinical school, thereby opening him up to criticism from all other sides. Jesus' answer, however, proves his fidelity to both the Jewish tradition and to a spirituality that transcends the legal interpretations of the Torah: the "second" commandment is the manifestation of the first. If we love the Lord God with our whole being, that love will manifest itself in our feeding of hungry, our sheltering the homeless, our liberating the oppressed. "To love your neighbor as yourself" is not confined to our "own" people or to a list of specific situations, but should affect every relationship we have and every decision we make. Every one of us, at one time or other, is an alien, outsider, foreigner and stranger.

As our society becomes more and more diverse, as science continues to make once unimaginable advances in all forms of technology, the ethical and moral questions we face become more complicated, difficult and challenging. The Great Commandment gives us the starting point for dealing with such issues: to love as God loves us — without limit, without condition, without counting the cost, completely and selflessly. In our e-connected existence, the words of Jesus in today's Gospel are especially challenging: to love with our whole heart and soul and mind requires us to "unplug" and be present to one another, to engage one another as our loving God is engaged with us, to seek not just images and perceptions of compassion but behold compassion and experience love in one another.

In the Common lectionary, today's Gospel from Matthew continues with another confrontation between Jesus and the Jewish leaders — only, this time, Jesus provokes the issue. The long-awaited Messiah, Israel believed, would be a "son of David." Referring to Psalm 110, Jesus asks how can David call someone who is his son "Lord" (*kyrios*)? The Pharisees have no answer. The point is that the Messiah of God in the person of Jesus is much more than the dynastic "king" Israel longs for to restore their political and economic fortunes.

*F*ather, you are the Source and Center of our lives.
By the light of your Word,
may we realize our "connectedness" to you,
    and through you, to one another.
May we be embraced by your compassion
in the love we extend to one another;
may we be reconciled with you
in our forgiveness of one another;
may we be worthy to be your sons and daughters
by honoring every human being
    as our brother and sister.

Sunday 31 / Proper 26

" … Do and observe whatever the scribes and Pharisees tell
you, but do not follow their example. For they preach but
do not practice. They tie up heavy burdens hard to carry and
lay them on people's shoulders, but they will not lift a finger
to move them. All their works are performed to be seen …
"The greatest among you must be your servant. All who exalt
themselves will be humbled, but all who humble themselves
will be exalted."

Matthew 23: 1–12

One hundred conductors

A few years ago, a group of young musicians from the
United States went to Havana to perform with the National Youth
Orchestra of Cuba. A Cuban and an American musician sat at
each stand. The combined philharmonic would play two pieces
— one conducted by the Cuban director and the second by the
American director.

The first piece was a colorful and brilliant composition written by the Cuban conductor. On the first day of rehearsal, the
conductor started working with the combined orchestra, but it
was soon clear that the complex Cuban rhythms of the piece were
so unfamiliar to the Americans that it was beyond them. First
concerned, then frustrated, finally resigned to failure, the Cuban
conductor declared from the podium, "I'm afraid that this is not
going to work. We have to cancel the performance."

But his American counterpart immediately leapt to the stage
and said to the young Cuban players through an interpreter, "Your
job is to teach these rhythms to your stand partner." And to his
own American players, he said, "Just give yourselves over to the
leaders sitting next to you. You will get the support you need."

The Cuban maestro began again. What happened startled everyone in the hall. The Cuban musicians were energized, exuberantly conducting their American counterparts with their instruments. The American musicians began to play the rhythms the way they were meant to be played. At the end of the piece, the Cuban conductor smiled and nodded — everything would be fine.

Next, the American conductor took the podium. He would lead the orchestra in Leonard Bernstein's fiendishly difficult masterpiece, the overture to the musical *Candide*. The piece, largely unknown in Cuba, was so difficult to play that the American orchestra sent the music to the Cubans three months earlier. But as he was about to rehearse the piece for the first time, the American conductor was told no music had ever arrived.

The blood drained from the American's face. It had taken his orchestra months to master *Candide*. But seeing the smiles on the American players' faces, he knew what to do. They reversed the process that had been so successful earlier in the rehearsal. Now the Americans were the enthusiastic conductors supporting the conscientious and committed Cuban players.

The concert was magnificent, led not by one distant figure at the podium, but by one hundred individual conductors teaching and supporting one another.[13]

When each musician took on the role of conductor and fulfilled that role with kindness, understanding and a commitment to the common good, the young members of the orchestra mirrored Christ's vision of faithful leadership and the greatness of humble service. Real authority is not a matter of power or wealth but is centered in the realization that our gifts and talents are a sacred trust given to us for the good of all; greatness in the reign of God is to put ourselves and our abilities at the service of the music we can create in concert with one another.

In today's pericope Jesus again challenges the detached, legalistic observance of the scribes and Pharisees, particularly the emptiness of their strict adherence to ritual. The scribes were the religious intellectuals of the time, skilled in interpreting the Law and applying it to everyday life; the Pharisees belonged to a religious fraternity ("the separated brethren") who prided themselves on the exact, meticulous observance of the Law. Jesus denounces their failure to live up to their teachings: In their eagerness to be revered, they dominate rather than to serve. Religious ostentation and pretension are rejected in favor of the Christian ideal of leadership contained in loving service to the community.

In the Gospel scheme of things, the greatest leaders and teachers are those who share their vision of faith not in words alone but by the power and authority of their example, in the integrity of their lives, in their commitment of service toward and respect for those in their charge. In warning his disciples not to use the titles "Rabbi," "Teacher" and "Father," Jesus condemns the spirit of pride and superiority such titles connote. Those who serve as teachers and leaders should be humbled by the fact that they are not teachers or leaders in their own right but by the inspiration and grace of God. In the reign of God, those who exercise authority have a particular responsibility to lead by serving.

For the person of faith, joy is found not in the recognition or honor that one receives in doing good but in the act of doing good itself, in realizing that we imitate Christ in such service, in the assurance that we are bringing the love of God into the lives of others.

*L*ord Jesus,
   may we seek to imitate your spirit of humble service
      to others.
   Help us to realize our life's purpose in doing the work
      of your Gospel.
   Let us discover our self-worth in our service to others.
   Make us great in our ability to forgive
      and seek forgiveness,
   experts in the building of peace and community,
   authorities in the ethics of justice and righteousness,
   teachers of selfless compassion and generosity.
   May humility be our dignity;
   may your glory be our exaltation.

Sunday 32 / Proper 27

"The kingdom of heaven will be like ten virgins who took their lamps and went out to meet the bridegroom. Five of them were foolish, and five were wise. The foolish ones, when taking their lamps, brought no oil with them, but the wise brought flasks of oil with their lamps ... Stay awake, for you know neither the day nor the hour."

Matthew 25: 1–13

"Like sands in an hour glass ... "

There once was a little girl who lived near the beach. She had a grandfather she loved very much and always looked forward to visiting him. Her grandfather had a collection of hourglasses and she delighted in turning them upside down and watching the sand sift through the glass bulbs.

She asked her grandfather why he had all of those hourglasses. Because, he explained, the glasses of sand reminded him that time was the most precious thing in the world.

Christmas was coming and the little girl had not seen her Grandpa for weeks. Eventually her mother was able to help her understand that Grandpa was in the hospital because he was very sick and that he might die. The little girl wasn't sure what death was. Her mother explained that life was like one of Grandpa's hourglasses and that Grandpa had very little time left.

One morning her mother told her daughter that they would be going to visit Grandpa that afternoon and asked her to make some kind of special Christmas present for him. The girl excitedly went to work on her gift.

When they got to the hospital, the little girl gave her grandfather a beautifully wrapped box. Her grandfather slowly unwrapped the box and looked inside and smiled. He understood immediately.

His granddaughter had filled the box with sand.

Oh, were it that easy: to simply extend our days by adding more sand to our hourglasses, more pages to our calendars, more turns to our watch's crystals. But, alas, the amount of time we are given by God is fixed at a set number of grains of sand, a set number of calendar squares, a set number of turns of the hands of the clock. Too often we fall into the mindset of the five "foolish" bridesmaids of today's Gospel: We live our lives in the false belief that we will always have time "later" to accomplish what we want our lives to be; we work ourselves to exhaustion and isolation, foolishly thinking that someday we will have "enough."

These last Sundays of the year focus on the *Parousia,* the Lord's return at the end of time. The parable of the bridesmaids, found only in Matthew's Gospel, is taken from Jesus' fifth and final discourse in Matthew, the great eschatological discourse. According to Palestinian custom, the bridegroom would go to the bride's house on their wedding day to finalize the marital agreement with his father-in-law. When the bridegroom would return to his own home with his bride, the bridesmaids would meet them as they approached, signaling the beginning of the wedding feast.

The image of the approaching wedding feast is used by Jesus to symbolize his coming at the end of time. Jesus' return will take many by complete surprise. The love we have for others as evidenced in works of kindness and compassion is the "oil" we store in our lamps awaiting for Christ's return.

The parable of the foolish virgins calls us to see our lives as preciously short and fragile, to realize that now is the time to seek the justice and compassion of God for ourselves and for those we love. Instead of terrifying us or intimidating us or driving us to despair, the inevitability of the return of Christ "the Bridegroom" should make us realize the preciousness of the gift of time we have been given and inspire us to make the most of the limited "sand" in our hourglasses.

*W*ith lamps lighted by the oil of your Word,
we await your coming, O Lord,
to take our places at the great wedding feast
in the Father's house.
In these precious days we have until then,
may our lives be illuminated by the light of your grace
so that we may reflect your complete and total love
    for all.

Sunday 33 / Proper 28

"'You wicked, lazy servant! So you knew that I harvest where I did not plant and gather where I did not scatter ... ?'
"For to everyone who has, more will be given, and they will grow rich; but from those who have not, even what they have will be taken away."

Matthew 25: 14–30

Every child's future ... if ...

*I*magine a classroom of eight- and nine-year-old children in any elementary school in any town.

See the boy in the third row who watches the clouds all day? He's not daydreaming — he's fascinated by weather: he wants to know why it rains, what makes it snow, how hurricanes form. As he gets older he could transform his inquisitiveness into a career as a meteorologist or science — *if ...*

Or the little girl in the fifth row? She is naturally loving, generous and kind. She helps her mom — a single parent — take care of her younger brother and sister. At such a young age, she has already discovered the joy of being a big sister. Some day she could be a compassionate teacher, a wise counselor, a skilled pediatrician, a loving mom — *if ...*

Every child in that classroom has the potential to do great things on any and every stage — from the laboratory to the board room, from the studio to the halls of government. This girl could create the next Microsoft; that boy may find the cure to cancer. They are limited only by their imaginations and the opportunities they will have to learn and grow. The possibilities for these bright, curious, enthusiastic students are endless — *if ...*

... *if* they are willing to take the risks that come with the gifts and talents they have been given ... *if* they invest the time, the energy, the hard work, the humility to learn and to try … *if* they commit themselves to their studies and training …

Every one of us — child or adult, student or teacher — has been entrusted by God with gifts and talents to contribute to the work of creation. The challenge is to be willing to risk exposing our true selves, to risk involvement with others, to risk failure, despair and ridicule. Jesus urges us not to "bury" our talents in the safe ground of self-interest and passivity but to "invest" them for the benefit of all. God will hold us accountable for what we have done with what we have been given. Christ calls us to a faith that is willing to take the risk of investing what we have in the greater good, and he promises us the grace to work to enable others to realize a return on the investment of their own talents in God's kingdom in our midst.

The "measure" of Christ's judgment in the world to come is made clear in the parable of the talents: The Lord will judge us according to how well we used the "talents" and gifts every one of us has been given. The greater the "capital" we have been given, the greater God's expectations.

Each one of us is given many opportunities to "reap and gather." The challenge of the Gospel is to be ready and willing to respond to those opportunities joyfully and generously for the sake of others, to build the kingdom of God in our own time and place. Whatever degree of talent, ability and wealth we possess have been "entrusted" to us by the "Master." Our place in the reign of God will depend on our stewardship of those gifts from God.

Christ calls us to a faith that is willing to take the risk of investing what we have in the greater good, and he promises us the grace to work to enable others to realize a return on the investment of their own talents in God's kingdom in our midst.

You have entrusted to us, O God,
   many gifts and blessings —
some we don't even realize that we possess.
Open our eyes with the light of gratitude
to realize all you have given us
and transform our hearts in your love
that we might give willingly and completely of those gifts
in order to reap and gather the harvest of your kingdom
in our own time and place.

Christ the King /
Reign of Christ [Proper 29]

"Come, you who are blessed by my Father. Inherit the kingdom prepared for you from the foundation of the world. For I was hungry and you gave me food, I was thirsty and you gave me drink, a stranger and you welcomed me …
"Whatever you did for one of the least brothers and sisters of mine, you did for me."

Matthew 25: 31—46

Christ in the parish

*J*im had moved into the Chicago parish a few years before. He never registered, never got a box of envelopes, never joined a parish committee, rarely spoke more than a few words to anyone.

And yet, his presence had a powerful impact on the whole parish.

Jim was your basic homeless street person. Actually, he had two homes. One was a bus bench near the church; the second was a back pew of the parish church — whenever the weather got too cold for his bus bench, Jim moved into the pew.

Jim was a stubborn and difficult man. He never panhandled. He refused any monies offered, often without uttering a word. Jim didn't make you feel good about being good. He neither smoked nor drank nor used drugs. He suffered from schizophrenia, causing him to withdraw from reality and exhibit erratic emotional and intellectual behavior. Unshaven and unwashed, he smelled like rancid chicken and had developed a haunting stare that made eye contact all but impossible.

But Jim was vivid testimony to this society's unsolved problems and unkept promises. His presence caused the priests of the parish to take measure of their priesthood. Just by his presence and powerful

---

silence he became a catalyst for meaningful action in the parish. His silent homily compelled people to become involved with the homeless of the neighborhood. People looked at Jim and wanted to do something. He probably flushed out more volunteers than a hundred bulletin pleas. Jim's presence was largely responsible for the parish's shelter program and soup kitchen.

Jim was only 58 when he died of leukemia, but he seemed a great deal older. At his funeral, the entire parish came to say goodbye to one of the most influential parishioners ever to attend their church.[15]

Christ is present in the Jims in our midst who call us beyond our own concerns and interests to see and serve Christ in them. Today's Gospel calls us to open our hands and hearts to them with the compassion and generosity of the God who promises to open his hands and heart to us.

Matthew's is the only description of the Last Judgment in any of the Gospels. It is Jesus' last discourse recorded by Matthew before the events of the Passion unfold. In the vision he presents in today's Gospel, Christ is the king who sits in judgment "as a shepherd separates sheep from goats." Christ the Shepherd-King clearly and unequivocally identifies himself with the poor. Compassion and charity will be the standards for determining one's entry into the future kingdom of God; our place in that kingdom will be determined by our ability to reach beyond ourselves to bring justice, peace and reconciliation into the lives of everyone.

Mother Teresa of Calcutta put today's Gospel theme so succinctly when she said: "At the end of life we will not be judged by how many diplomas we have received, how much money we have made, how many great things we have done. We will be judged by *I was hungry and you gave me to eat ... I was naked and you clothed me ... I was homeless and you took me in.* Hungry not only for bread — but hungry for love; naked not only of clothing — but naked of human dignity and respect; homeless not only for want of a room of bricks, but homeless because of rejection. This is Christ in distressing disguise."

Ordinary Time

*C*ompassionate God,
open our eyes to see your face in the faces
of the poor, the troubled and the forgotten;
open our hands to reach out to them in hope and peace.
May we give you thanks for all your blessings to us
by seeking to share those same blessings
with all of our brothers and sisters in Christ Jesus.

Notes

Christmas

1. Suggested by "A joy full of dust and dung" by Abbot John Klassen, O.S.B., *The Abbey Banner*, St. John's Abbey, Collegeville, Minn., Winter 2006.
2. From a sermon by Leslie Weatherhead, cited in "God's Arms" by Michael Lindvall, *The Christian Century*, June 1, 2004.
3. Adapted with permission from "Let's Hear It for the Child" by Mary O'Connell, *U.S. Catholic*, December 1997. Subcriptions: $22 year. *U.S. Catholic*, 205 West Monroe Street, Chicago IL 60606, 800/328-6515, www.uscatholic.org.
4. From *Letters from the Desert* by Carlo Carretto (Maryknoll, N.Y.: Orbis Books, 1972), pages 138–139.

Easter Triduum

1. LaVonne Platt, from the *More-With-Less Cookbook* by Doris Janzen Longacre, published by the Herald Press for the Mennonite Central Committee, Akron, Pennsylvania (1976).

Easter

1. Based on a sermon by M. Craig Barnes.
2. From "Knit Together with Prayer" by the Rev. Susan S. Izard, *Spirituality & Health,* November/December 2004.

Ordinary Time

1. From "Staying power" by James Howell, *The Christian Century,* October 30, 2007. Copyright 2007 by *The Christian Century.* Reprinted with permission. Subscriptions: $49 per year from *The Christian Century,* Post Office Box 1941, Marion OH 43306, 800/208-4097.]
2. *For Better or For Worse* by Lynn Johnston, October 26, 1995 (United Press Syndicate).
3. From "Lost & Found" by Sue Norton, *Commonweal*, January 18, 2008.
4. *Newsweek*, June 11, 1998.
5. "My Turn: A Doctor's Dilemma — Helping an accident victim on the road could land you in court" by James N. Dillard, M.D., *Newsweek*, June 12, 1995.
6. From *Make Me an Instrument of Your Peace* by Kent Nerburn (Harper San Francisco, 1999), pages 114–116.
7. "The Perils of Freedom" by Jens Soering, *America*, July 5–12, 2004.
8. *Overcoming Life's Disappointments* by Harold S. Kushner (New York: Alfred A. Knopf, 2006), page 35.
9. *Gilead* by Marilynne Robinson (New York: Farrar, Strauss and Giroux, 2004), pages 19, 42.
10. *To Begin Again: The Journey Toward Comfort, Strength and Faith in Difficult Times* by Naomi Levy (New York: Alfred A. Knops, 1998), page 142.

11. From "Voices from Ground Zero" by Courtney V. Cowart, *Spirituality and Health*, Fall 2002.

12. *Bird by Bird: Some Instructions on Writing and Life* by Anne Lamott (New York: Pantheon Books, 1994), page 205.

13. From *The Art of Possibility* by Rosamund Stone Zander and Benjamin Zander (New York: Penguin Books, 2002), pages 74-76.

14. As told by Rob Gilbert, PhD.

15. Adapted with permission from "The Unsightly guest who taught a parish how to see" by Tim Unsworth, *Salt*, June 1988. Published by the Claretians, 205 West Monroe Street, Chicago IL 60606, 312/236–7782, www.salt.claretianpubs.org.